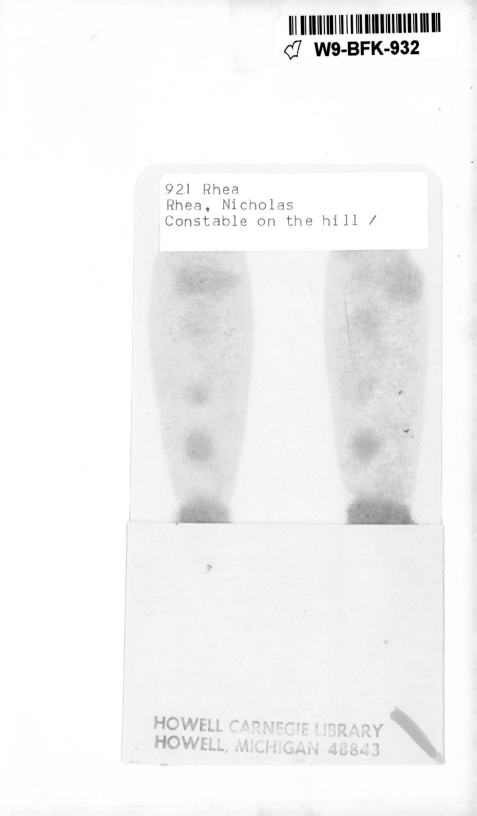

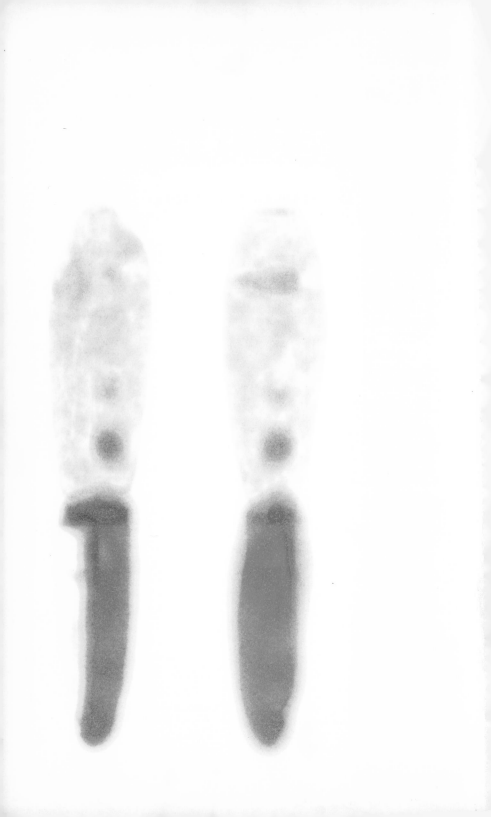

CONSTABLE ON THE HILL

Constable on the Hill

NICHOLAS RHEA

ST. MARTIN'S PRESS
NEW YORK

© Nicholas Rhea 1979
First published in the United States
of America 1979

St. Martin's Press, Inc.,
175 Fifth Avenue
New York, N.Y. 10010

Library of Congress Catalog Number 79-83824

ISBN 0-312-16439-4

Printed in Great Britain

One

The police house at Aidensfield in North Yorkshire occupies what is probably the most beautiful site in the country. High on an escarpment overlooking Ryedale, it surveys two valleys, one to the back and the other to the front, with its own finger of land neatly dividing them. It is a detached house, built of local yellow stone, and boasts a garage, an office and extensive views to the south, east and north, with moderate views to the west. It stands alone on its hill top, a sentinel for all to note and there is nothing around it save green grass, deciduous trees and oceans of fresh moorland air laced with the multifarious scents of rural England.

Looking north from the rear bedroom window, one sees the three white radomes of Fylingdales Ballistic Missile Early Warning Station, like a clutch of duck eggs sitting among the heather, the gorgeous autumn purple of those distant moors, and the lush greenery of Ryedale with its host of tiny communities. To the east stands the tiny Minster of Thackerston and beyond that, the coast; on a clear day, it is possible to imagine the North Sea off Scarborough but distance and blue hazes can confuse the eye and baffle the brain. Is that blue really the sea or is it just a blue haze? It doesn't matter – it is attractive and therefore worthy of interest.

To the south is a smaller valley with a farm seemingly at one's feet, for it lies just over the fringe of trees at the foot of the garden. Beyond are the wooded hills lined with rows of regimented larch and spruce trees. Down on the flat valley floor are more small communities of farms and people. To the west, the view is not so extensive, for the policeman's hill continues to rise, taking its metalled road to the heights of the Hambleton Hills and then to Sutton Bank with its high-

5

flying gliders. From that supreme vantage point, one can look across the vast vale of York, described by Chevalier Bunsen as "the most beautiful and romantic vale in the world, the Vale of Normandy excepted". The lower York-shire Dales lead skywards towards the Pennines which form a fitting and rugged backcloth to this land of castles and abbeys, rivers and roads, villages and heights.

This piece of England, called Romantic Ryedale by its inhabitants, is famous to those people as "God's own country". They worship the place. It contains everything for the country-lover: wildlife in all its forms, centuries of stirring history, folklore and legends, fascinating people, a local dialect, and a landscape comprising some of the most panoramic and impressive views in the whole of England. My police house commands one of those views.

It was to this area, therefore, that I came one summer day. It must be said that I had not come from choice, for I had been posted to Aidensfield as its new village policeman. With my wife Mary and my family of three tiny children, I had driven from our old home and arrived an hour or so ahead of the removal van with its meagre load of our sparse belongings.

After only five years of marriage and with five mouths to feed, we had very little furniture, but a lack of possessions was a great comfort to a policeman in a county police force. My liability to be posted to far-flung locations meant I did not buy objects like fitted carpets or expensive curtains. Instead, all county policemen acquired functional furnishings like tables which folded into corners, chairs which were easily portable, beds which were not four-posters and small square carpets that would sit anywhere and be complementary to almost any wallpaper.

On that removal day, we had packed a picnic and I reckoned we would arrive at our new house around lunch-time; we decided to picnic there. Over the final miles, I drove through Maddleskirk with its impressive Benedictine abbey, then found myself in Aidensfield. This is a beautiful village, built snugly into a steep hillside so that no northern wind can chill its homes. The southern sun warms them all and the spring daffodils bloom three weeks ahead of those in less

congenial climes, like my hill top. I passed through Aidensfield very slowly, looking at the squat parish church, the
ultra-modern Catholic church, the friendly pub, the garage
and the village shop, all within a hundred yards of one
another. One or two people pottered along that peaceful
street, and I wondered if they realised that the battered old
Hillman cruising suspiciously slowly contained their new
bobby.

Once up the steep hill at the distant end of Aidensfield, I
turned right and there, standing magnificently on its own
hill-top site, was that lovely police house. It was ten minutes
to one, and the children were as excited as a three-year-old, a
two-year-old and a one-year-old could be.

I steered the gallant old vehicle through the open gate of
the police house and halted on the concrete drive. The house
was empty, of course, the previous occupants having been
moved out that same morning. Happily, the day was fine and
dry, but many is the time policemen have moved house
during rain or snow, to suffer the indignity of wet-footed
removal men tramping all over clean floors. We were very
fortunate to have such a lovely day in June.

The key, I had previously been told, would be concealed in
the garage, under a half-full tin of paint. I found it, and from
the attached label, saw it was for the front door. By now, the
children were pottering about the spacious lawn, exploring
their new territory with a curiosity that could lead to problems, but Mary decided to leave them there, took the key and
together we approached our front entrance.

We were surprised to find a cabbage in a string bag
hanging from the door knob. Mary looked at me for guidance
and I looked at the cabbage. It seemed a good solid cabbage,
but there was no note and no indication of its *raison d'être*.
Initially, I suspected some form of skullduggery, and therefore
decided to examine the other doors before taking further
action. Was it full of sneezing powder or water? Was it a
plastic one? I advised Mary to keep well away from the object
and made my way to the back door, leading into the kitchen.
It was located in a passage, access to which was through an
outer door next to the garage. This was not locked, so I
opened it, turned towards the kitchen and found a brace of

wood pigeons hanging from that door knob. Then, on the office door, was a monster of a hare. As we would say in Yorkshire dialect, it was a "greeat awd ram-cat of a heeare".

I knew of the age-old custom of giving presents to country policemen, but here was I, on my very first day at Aidensfield, with presents all around me, and not a single hint as to their origins. Having discovered the fur and feather, I accepted the cabbage for what it was – a useful gift. It was a lovely welcome. I unlocked the door and with due solemnity, carried Mary across the threshold and the children followed, shouting and running about the entrance hall and ground-floor rooms in sheer exuberance. They'd have to stop that caper when the van arrived.

To the right of the entrance hall was the door into my office; the office had a door leading into the garden but that was seldom used. Most of the callers came to the front door of the house. The office had a counter across the middle with shelves beneath it and in the centre was an official looking desk and telephone.

The house was in a state of complete cleanliness, thanks to the outgoing couple and we could move straight in. On the left immediately inside the door was the staircase and already two of the youngsters were scrambling noisily up the bare wooden steps. Jane was too young to attempt such feats so she accompanied Mary and me as we examined the house. The dining-room had a plain-looking electric fire and a window looking south; next to it was the lounge with a fireplace for coal blazes, and a window looking south. Those views were glorious, taking in an entire valley with conifers beyond, scattered farms below and the distant wolds of the East Riding of Yorkshire.

The kitchen was unbelievably tiny and there was an ancient coke boiler in one corner with a pantry beneath the stairs. The kitchen door led out into the back passage near the garage, where I'd found the pigeons. Upstairs, were two reasonable bedrooms, with windows looking south, plus a smaller one with windows looking north, and a bathroom – with windows looking north.

A big garden with soft fruit, vegetables and flowers sloped away from the house on its southern aspect, just beyond the lawn underneath the lounge and dining-room windows. There would be about one-third of an acre of garden, much of it allowed to go to waste but about a quarter of which had been cultivated. Our June arrival meant we gained from the work of others – sometimes, you won, sometimes you lost! An attractive rockery edged the lawn at the front, but the lawn extended completely around the house which meant the children could gallop around and around in ever-decreasing circles. It was a marvellous way to tire them for bed and to occupy them as the men unloaded our belongings.

We enjoyed our picnic on the lawn, sitting on the shorn grass and gazing south across my new beat. I could see farmers working in the fields, cars moving in the distance with sun glinting from their glass, trees swaying in a gentle breeze and rooks soaring high above in the clear sky. There were the summer sounds of an unseen tractor, the constant hum of bees at work nearby and the voice of a skylark on high. We sat there for about an hour, thoroughly enjoying those precious moments of peace.

I was reminded of the words of William Shenstone who wrote:

> Devoid of hate, devoid of strife,
> Devoid of all that poisons life.

Then the removal men arrived.

It was evident that they had sampled some of the local ale *en route* for they arrived at our house in a benevolent mood, albeit determined to be unpacked and away before five that afternoon. Because the road ran directly past my front gate, the driver, a squat man with two or three days growth of beard, decided he would reverse his vehicle into my gateway. This would enable our furniture to be emptied onto the concrete forecourt of the garage, and thus make it easier to carry indoors. I thought it a sound idea and moved my car into the garage beside my official motor-cycle. So far, so good. We decided that the carpets must be first into the house because once they were in position, the removal men would place the larger items wherever we decided.

The driver, whose name I never knew, began to manoeuvre his huge vehicle backwards towards my gate. It was a narrow

gate, even for the passage of a family car, and was most
definitely not designed for the antics of reversing pantech-
nicons. The driver, however, seemed very confident that he
could squeeze its bulk through the gap, while his mate, the
thinnest man I've ever seen, leapt out and began to shout
directions. By darting backwards and forwards, he encour-
aged the lumbering lorry to inch its way towards my gate
posts. I issued the inevitable warnings, but the lorry hit both
gateposts, as I knew it must; it did so in spite of the driver's
confidence, and in spite of the mate's incomprehensible
shouts. My yells were ignored.

It didn't stop there. It came on. The rear wheels crunched
across the remains of the posts and smashed the fallen gates
into matchwood. Only when the rear was some twelve feet
into my garden, did the driver stop.

"That's better," he said, leaping from his cab. "Now we
can get cracking."

"Look there!" I shouted, pointing to the mangled gates and
their accessories. "Smashed . . . the sergeant will play hell
with me . . . I'm new here."

"Forget it, son," said the driver. "We've moved every
bobby into this house since it was built, and we always smash
the gates down. It's t'only way to get in. And it gets you a set
o' new gates every three years or so. Good logic that – the
insurance will see to it. Good thing, insurance."

"The insurance will see you all right," said the thin one,
and with no more ado, they got to work. They worked most
efficiently, unloading our meagre, battered belongings and
positioning them in the house under Mary's instructions. She
brewed the inevitable cups of tea and they dropped the
inevitable mirror and crockery, excusing themselves by saying, "The insurance will see you all right."

Somehow, a key to the wardrobe was lost, which the
insurance would see to, and one of the bedroom windows got
cracked, while they were manoeuvring a dressing-table into
position. The insurance would see to that, I was told. They
unloaded the larger items more quickly than we could determine their position so when a backlog occurred, they stopped
and drank tea. That was when we made decisions about the
location of our furnishings which would prevail until we left

this house with the assistance of another furniture wagon and its insurers.

Sometimes the lanky one, whose name I learned was Sid, would stop and admire a recently acquired piece of furniture. For example, after unloading our radiogram, the pair of them placed it on the ground, walked around it and Sid said, "You've come on since last time, eh?"

This pair had apparently moved us into our previous house, four years earlier, and now took an opportunity to comment upon the proliferation of children and the acquisition of new furniture and other belongings. During one of our many breaks for tea, and with the children getting in the way, I asked Sid how he'd remembered us from all the other policemen he'd moved around the North Riding.

"That bloody piano," he motioned with his head towards the wagon. My piano was still aboard.

I laughed at the memory. The piano was gigantic with a solid iron frame. It was a Broadwood and therefore a useful instrument. It had been a twenty-first birthday present to me, having belonged to my grandparents. Because we could not accommodate it in our very first home at Strensford, it had remained at my grandparents' home until we made our first move to more suitable premises. It had been impossible to get it into the Strensford police house because of winding steps and narrow passages. Upon our move from there, we had arranged for a local garage to store the piano overnight on the eve of our transfer; we would collect it the following morning. We did that. The ivory-toothed monster demanded every skill known to those strong men, but after much panting and heaving, they got it aboard their removal van, shut the tail-board and off we went. Upon our arrival at North-allerton, the piano was first off the lorry. The men placed it on the footpath outside that suburban house, and its wheels promptly sank into the macadam which surfaced the path. It sank the full depth of those small metal wheels; retrieval was messy and tricky and its marks remained for many years as a monument to our presence there. Getting it into that house had been a further problem; it sat outside in the rain until the very last minute, when finally, after much cursing and debating, we managed to inch it inside.

Having got it inside that house, we breathed a sigh of relief – and then remembered we'd left Mary's bicycle at Strensford, outside the garage which had kindly stored the piano. We'd placed it there while we lifted the piano aboard, and had forgotten all about it. I rang a friend at the police station and he took the cycle into protective custody until we could collect it. We never did collect it – perhaps it's still there, in the cell passage?

For those reasons, therefore, the piano lingered in the memories of these removal men. Now that Sid had mentioned it, I began to wonder if we would get it into this house. The entrance hall was very narrow and short, and that instrument demanded lots of space and massive strength. The strength was there in those sinewy bodies, but space? I could always keep it in the garage.

The piano was taken off the lorry and left on the garage forecourt until everything else was inside the house. The children did their best, losing things, carrying things, getting in the way and falling into and over everything. By four-thirty, the van was empty the house was full and we had a cup of tea. Only the piano remained.

Using a little trolley, they steered it towards the front door and Sid measured up the prospects with his eyes.

"Nay," he said. "It'll not go in."

"It'll have to," I said in what must have been a pleading tone. "It can't stay on the lawn."

"It'll mean taking it to bits." He leaned on the lid. "Piece by piece, with screwdrivers. It'll be a long job, and it'll never be right again. Bad to tune are pianos that have been taken to bits."

"But overtime for you, eh?" I smiled.

"Aye, happen," he grinned.

But his mate wasn't interested in overtime. "We can do it if that front door comes off," he said. "Take t'front off t'piano, an' all. It'll sidle round that banister end, and go in."

"You and your bloody piano," Sid growled at me. "Why do you have to cart a thing that size around with you?"

"I can't live without it," I told him. "It's part of my life!"

"You bloody pianists are all alike – kinky. Why don't you play summat like a flute?"

I didn't tell him that I couldn't play a note. I daren't tell him, not now. I'd always wanted to play a piano, ever since I was a small boy, but somehow never found the time, even if I had found the instrument. I had learned the violin and the recorder, but had always hankered after the piano. I had therefore asked for this one as my twenty-first birthday present because it belonged to the family and because it might otherwise be sold. All those years after moving into Aidensfield, I still have the piano and it continues to cause problems whenever we move house. And I still cannot play it.

By removing the front door and by sheer brute strength and skill, those men got it inside the house and somehow reached the lounge.

"It's not damaged," they said, proudly.

"It's a good job it isn't!" I said, "It would have been a big insurance job."

"That's it, then," Sid announced. "All in. Report the gateposts to your sergeant and write to my firm about the breakages. Insurance jobs, all of them."

I gave them a tip, said farewell until next time and watched them take the lorry away from the house. I was left with two broken gates and three children who couldn't wait to get onto the road. Until now, the lorry's front end had effectively blocked this exit, but I managed to stand up the gates by propping them against old packing cases, then Mary and I set about the massive task of putting the house straight.

We were allowed one day off duty before a removal, a day for the removal and one day off duty afterwards. That's all – after that, it was work as normal. By half-past-five, the children were beyond themselves with fatigue and hunger, so Mary made us a meal. We bathed them and plonked them into their beds, thankful that they, at least, were no longer a liability.

Then we turned our attention to the packing cases and began the long task of finding somewhere to put everything. We turned in just after midnight, completely exhausted and the children woke us next morning at six. We struggled, aching, from our beds and began another long day's work. The tasks seemed without end, but several villagers telephoned during the day, just to welcome us. I had no idea who they were. All of them said, "Welcome," and all said, "We'll be meeting you soon." It helped us through that tiring day. No one acknowledged leaving the cabbage, the pigeons or the hare, but already I began to feel at home. It did not take too long to make the house habitable, and besides, county policemen of those times never unpacked everything, in case they were soon on the move.

Like those men, I maintained a useful collection of empty and half-full tea-chests which I lodged in garages and attics. Sometimes, we received only one week's notice of a removal to a new station, sometimes less, therefore we remained ready for instant exit. Happily, things have changed but at that time, I decided to position my tea-chests in the office.

The phone rang during the late afternoon of that first day, and a voice said,

"Rhea?"

"Yes?" I answered.

"Sergeant Blaketon here. I'm your section sergeant. I'm at Ashfordly. You're on at nine in the morning. Spend the first hour in your own office, finding things. Check the inventory. Then get the bike out and come down here. Be here before half-past-ten. Right?"

"Yes, Sergeant," I heard myself say, and the phone died.

He didn't ask if I could ride the official motor-cycle and I didn't know either, so I went into the garage to examine it. There was plenty of room for my car and the bike. It was a Francis Barnett two-stroke with a windscreen at the front and a radio on the back. A tall, flexible aerial protruded from the rear, like an upright tail, and the speaker was fixed to the handlebars, just above the tank. The entire machine was black and very clean, so I sat astride. I shook it and found it was full of petrol, kicked the starter and it burst immediately into life in the confines of the garage. I chugged outside, did a shaky tour of the lawn much to the amusement of my family and returned it to its place in the garage. I had ridden a motor-cycle as a teenager but had rapidly decided on a car after Mary and I ploughed through a hedge on our old machine. That incident put me off work for eight weeks.

But now I must ride again. On a summer's day, it would be very pleasant and I was looking forward to it. My gear was in the office, including a crash helmet of the correct size. Waterproof leggings and several coats completed the outfit, all sent along ahead of me by our efficient Clothing Department. I wondered how it would feel to ride a motor-cycle in police uniform. There's a certain difference between roaring along on one's own machine at the age of nineteen and steering a police motor-cycle about its legitimate business. I would soon know that difference.

At seven the following morning, the children earned their keep by waking us, and I dressed and shaved. I put on a smart uniform and breakfasted, then went into my little office well before eight-thirty. I searched the drawers of the desk and found a mileage book for the motor-cycle. This had to be completed after every journey and after every filling of the petrol tank. I found the inventory for the house and office, checked it and found everything there. Also in the office were files of offence reports, the work of my predecessor, files full of circulars bearing details of unsolved local and national crimes, and masses of other papers. There were leaflets about warble fly, anthrax and foul pest, about firearms and vehicle accidents, about Colorado beetles and police dances. And there was the Beat Report.

This was a most useful compilation, for it was an encyclopaedia of information appertaining to that beat. It provided me with the names of people like doctors, vets, RSPCA officials, Water Board officials, Gas Board and electrical wizards. It told me who to trust and who to watch; it named local villains and ne'er-do-wells; it had phone numbers of important institutions like the garages and pubs, and it listed churches, schools, experts on sundry things and a whole host of other useful material.

As I browsed through its pages, the phone rang.

"P.C. Rhea," I answered, somewhat nervously, for this could be my first job, my first piece of live duty.

"It's Alwyn Foxton down at Ashfordly," came the voice. "Pleased to make your acquaintance. You're coming in, Serge tells me, to have a look around this office?"

"Yes, about half-ten."

"There's a lot of messages for you," he said. "Routine stuff – stolen vehicles, wanted and missing persons, housebreakings and larcenies. That sort of thing. Nothing urgent."

"I'll pick it up when I get in, eh?"

"Fine. See you then."

And he rang off.

From this point, I knew I was doing real police work. After spending the past four years in an office, working with filing systems, accounts and housing problems, it was refreshing and exciting to return to real police work. Out here on one's own, there was no knowing what lay around the corner, no idea what was going to happen during the next day, next hour or even next minute. I was on duty twenty-four hours a day, although I worked a basic eight hours per day. That did not prevent me from being knocked out of bed at any time to deal with anything, even on my official day off. But that kind of life has its compensations, like freedom to patrol the beat as one wishes, freedom to mix with the people of the area and freedom to make one's own decisions, plus the thrill of finding cabbages on door knobs.

By ten o'clock, I had found my way around the office and had discovered the whereabouts of everything I needed. I found the switch for the heater, the key for the office door and the piece of chalk that every policeman carried in those days. It was used to mark the position of car wheels on the road surface when dealing with traffic accidents; it meant the cars could be moved before measurements were taken and so avoid congestion. I popped the chalk into my pocket, found a roll-up ruler too, had a cup of coffee and sallied forth into Ashfordly, four miles away.

I drove very steadily, the Francis Barnett wobbling alarmingly from time to time, and I forgot to switch on the police radio. But I got to Ashfordly without mishap and found the police station. I had to ask the way – I felt something of a fool, sitting on a police motor-cycle in full uniform, asking a little old lady the way to the police station. She told, but her eyes told of her alarm. She would tell a good tale over coffee that morning.

Ashfordly Police Station is a beautiful building. It is built of good-quality brick, and stands solidly on one of the nicer streets, just off the centre of this busy market town. Attached to each end of the office there is a police house, one being occupied by Sergeant Blaketon and the other by the senior constable, in this case Alwyn Foxton. In front of the station is an attractive garden, tidily kept by the sergeant or anyone else detailed to do so, while inside the place is immaculate. A daily cleaner pops in to do the brasses, to dust and polish and consequently the place reeks of polish and shines with the brilliance of a well-kept fire-engine. Police cleaning ladies are inordinately proud of their own buildings.

There is one garage and it was occupied by the official car, a neat black Ford Anglia. The place hummed with clean-cut efficiency.

I must admit that I trembled with anticipation as I walked along the path towards the front door. I had parked the motor-bike beside a convenient wall and entered to smell the cleanliness. I found a grey-haired policeman leaning on the counter, waiting for me with his red and jolly face.

"Alwyn Foxton," he extended a hand.

"Nicholas Rhea," I shook his hand.

"Sergeant Blaketon had to go out," he told me. "He won't be long. Take those leggings and things off, and I'll show you round. Not that there's much to see."

In fact, there was very little to see. To the left of the door was the tiny public office with a long wooden counter running from the inside of that door. To the right, was the sergeant's office. Alwyn explained there were two sergeants – Charlie Bairstow who was enjoying a day off and who lived at Brantsford, and Oscar Blaketon now on duty and somewhere in town. Bairstow was easy-going, he told me, while Blaketon stuck to the rules. I would meet them both in due course and make my own judgements.

The office contained bound copies of the *Criminal Law Review,* the *Justice of the Peace,* and some very ancient police law books. There was little else, save the weekly duty sheets. The duty sheet showed me as 'rural beat' for tomorrow and the following day, with a late route from 7 pm until 11 pm the day after that.

Alwyn showed me the Found Property register, the Lost Property register, the return of licensing premises, the return of explosives stores, bookmakers' shops, telephone calls register, postage book, the list of keyholders of places like banks and shops, and the names of local contacts. I would, from time to time, be instructed to perform duty in this town, and based on this office, especially when there was a shortage of men due to leave or sickness. In any case, I was expected to pop in at least twice a week to keep myself updated with affairs in town. Actually, the town boasted a population of only 3,000 but for us folks on the moors, this was a considerable centre of activity.

"Have we any cells?" I asked, thinking of prisoners.

"Two," Alwyn told me. "I'll show you. In fact," he went on, "the toilet is in one of the cells. We haven't an official toilet here, so we all use the cells."

He led me into the tiny cell passage where were confronted by two massive, studded doors with huge keys and gigantic iron hinges. No. 1 cell was on the left.

"Males in No. 1," he said. "Females in No. 2."

He pushed open the door of No. 1 and revealed the carcase of a fallow deer. It was lying on the stone floor.

"Killed in an accident with a milk lorry," he said. "This morning, just out of town."

"What happens to it?" I asked.

"We've an arrangement with a local hotel," he said.

"Arrangement?" I asked, wondering what sort of arrangement it could be.

"Oh, it's all above board," he smiled. "The deer about us, in the hills and forests, belong to the local estate, and his Lordship wants all those killed like this to be sent to the King's Head. He owns that hotel, by the way. When we've one brought in, we ring the hotel and the manager arranges collection. The estate gives us a useful donation for the Police Widows' Pension Fund. Deer are not reportable road accidents, as you know, but we take them in because too many bloody motorists insist on fetching them here. We get about two a week."

The deer's head, damaged on one side, lay on a piece of newspaper which absorbed the blood. There was the traditional wooden bed, boxed in all around, and a toilet in the corner. Nothing else furnished the place.

"Ladies in here," he said, throwing open the door of No. 2. This one was full of chrysanthemums. They stood around on the bed, the floor, on a board on top of the toilet basin, and on shelves which stood loosely against the walls. They were in all colours, shapes and sizes, and they were beautiful.

"Mine," said Alwyn, proudly. "That's ideal for them, especially when it's very hot outside. Lovely and cool in there. I grow them for showing, you know. Get prizes all over. Lovely flowers, eh?"

"Marvellous," I agreed, having never seen such a wealth of colour in a police cell. "But what happens if you arrest somebody? Where do you put your prisoners?"

"Arrest?" he sounded horrified. "We don't arrest people here!"

Two

Having made contact with my colleagues at Ashfordly Police Station, one of my first duties was to acquaint myself with the public of Aidensfield and the residents of the surrounding villages which formed my beat. These were country folk, down-to-earth people whose ancestors had occupied these moors for generations and who had a built-in suspicion of strangers. This was coupled with a bluntness that was typically Yorkshire and yet it hinted at absolute honesty and integrity. Being moor folk, they also possessed a natural hardiness and a desire never to tangle with newcomers to the area. They called newcomers "off cum'd 'uns".

I was conscious of this because I had been nurtured in such a village at the other side of the moors and was reminded of a policeman colleague who was posted to a remote village in the depths of the North Yorkshire moors. Some weeks after his arrival, he was walking through Whemmelby when a man hailed him. The other was a retired gentleman, judging by his appearance, for he had grey hair, a somewhat stooping stance and a terrier on a lead.

"Are you the new policeman?" he'd asked Les, conversationally.

"I am," Les had replied, smiling.

"Well, you'll have the devil's own job with 'em round here," the man had said. "I've lived in this village for over thirty years, and they still regard me as an outsider."

He wasn't joking either. It was with this in my mind that I began my tour of inspection. It was a goodwill tour of my beat, my first and vitally important public relations exercise. It wasn't easy finding an excuse to drop in on people who had no reason to know me and who weren't accustomed to uniformed police officers calling unannounced at their homes. I was fortunate in having a reason for calling at Low Mires Farm, on the outskirts of Crampton. This was my very first port of call.

I knocked on the door and a young woman answered; her pretty face wore that haunted look that people acquire when they open the door and find a policeman standing there. Has someone died, or are we in trouble? I smiled in the hope it would lessen the tension, removed my cap and said, "I've come about Mr Bradshaw's firearm certificate. It's due for renewal."

The girl looked me up and down, nodded and shouted, "Father!", and vanished inside, leaving me standing on the doorstep. After a long, silent wait, a tall gaunt man appeared. He must have been in his late sixties and wore carpet slippers which scuffed the sandstone passage as he walked. He used the walls as supports along his short journey and his face bore a day's white whiskers but his brown eyes were alive and intelligent, the only bright spot in his weathered appearance.

"And who might thoo be, lad?" He leaned against the door pillar, slightly out of breath. He studied me carefully, those brown eyes ranging the full length of my build.

"The new policeman, P.C. Rhea," I informed him. "I moved into the police house at Aidensfield a couple of days ago."

"Oh, aye?"

"Yes, and I've come about this," I waved the application form at him. "It's your firearm certificate, it's due for renewal."

"Aye, thoo'll be reet. Thoo'll be yan o' them townies, eh? Sent oot here ti mak us country folks larn t'laws."

"Well, I . . ."

"Thoo'll have been in t'office, eh? A scholar mebbe? All book larning and syke? A young feller gahin up t'stee, heading for promotion, eh?" (*Stee* is the North Riding dialect word for *ladder*.)

I had indeed been stationed in the Accounts Department of Force Headquarters at Northallerton, a small thriving market town, but for Mr Bradshaw, it seemed I was one of the dreaded townies, sent out here to harass him. I wondered if he thought I'd come from the south, too.

"I'm just a policeman," I tried, wondering if they were all like this character. I was still on the doorstep and realised his daughter was watching me. She remained at the distant end of the long, dark passage playing with the apron she wore. "Shall we fill this form in?"

"It's nut oft I allows strangers inti my parlour," he said, shaking his head solemnly. "We've nivver seen thoo afoore, lad. Nivver. Thoo's a stranger in theease parts, thoo sees."

"I'm the village policeman." I made another attempt to convince him I was honest and trustworthy, and ran a hand down my uniform to emphasise the point.

"That's mebbe so, but thoo's still a stranger ti us. Ah reckons nowt ti strangers."

"All right," I compromised. "We'll stand here and fill it in."

I produced a pen from my tunic pocket and continued, "I'll have to see your current certificate and your rifle. I've got to enter the number of it, and other details, in the renewal form. It's your rifle I'm interested in, not shot-guns."

"It seems ti be a lot of fuss about nowt," he grumbled, eyeing me carefully. "Syke a lot of form-filling in as nivver was. Will thoo fill it in for me? My awd hands is a bit crammly wi' t'rheumatics."

"Yes, of course," I assured him. "That's what I'm here for – to help you."

"Aye, but thoo's new ti theease parts, and I'm nut yan for letting strange folks . . ."

I tried another line of approach. For this, I relied heavily upon my own village upbringing. Having been brought up in the dialect of the North Yorkshire moors, I spoke it as my native tongue. I had learned to be 'slape-tongued' when I left for the outside world of Northallerton. I therefore looked at him, and then at the daughter who by this time had crept forward a few paces, still fiddling with her apron. I addressed them both.

"Leeakster, maister, Ah's nut 'ere ti be kept ootsahde, yakking ti thoo and thi dowter when there's wark ti be deean. If thoo dissn't git this form filled in, ah'll etti git ower that hill and back ti my desk, and then tell 'em up at oor head office that awd Bradshaw's as orkerd as pump-watter, and that he weearn't sign up."

"Come in, lad," he grinned suddenly, his face breaking into a wide smile. "By, Mary, git t'kettle on. This un's yan of us."

And from that moment, I was always welcome at Sam Bradshaw's farm, whether or not I was there on business. He always found time to talk while his Mary produced a cup of tea and a slice of home-made apple pie with fresh cream. She looked after the house because her mother had died some years ago, and I knew there was no prospect of her marrying. She was very pretty in a rural sort of way and was shy to the point of embarrassment. She'd be in her early thirties, I guessed, and would have made some man a fine wife.

It was a cosy farm, run in a carefree but efficient manner and eventually Sam Bradshaw learned that my father was secretary to a fishing club on the Yorkshire River Esk, a river renowed for its salmon and trout. Mr Bradshaw was a keen fisherman and I told him I could get him a day ticket when he fancied a trip across to the Esk. For a stranger, I was suddenly very acceptable, although he never did take that fishing trip. For him, it was a dream for the future, something to look forward to.

I found that my dialect was an asset in my daily work, especially when dealing with farmers like him who insisted on using it in my presence. Many of them talked in their broadest tongue when strangers were about, either to confuse or impress them, and this was particularly evident in the pubs. But I could talk about swingletrees, nabblings, jauping and dunderheads, black-locks and bletherskites, pleeafing and ploating, owersetten and underhanded, just like the folk hereabouts. I knew the meaning of local proverbs like "As prickly as a prickly-back otchen", "As soft-hearted as a rezzil", "As warm as a sheep net", "As lonely as a mile-stone", and I could appreciate the thoughtful sayings like, "Maist folk can see t'wrang they've deean, but nut t'wrang they're deeing," or "He's nobbut half-rocked 'at believes ivverything, but he's clean oot of his head 'at believes nowt."

The uniform was a great asset, of course. It was, and still is, respected in this locality and I soon found myself being able to talk with the locals on level terms. I was not regarded as a rule-bound troublemaker from afar, but a friend to whom they could turn. I respected their confidence in me, and realised the "official" blind-eye had to be turned from time to time. Warnings, not summonses, were utilised where possible.

One example of the type of dutiful assistance I was expected to give came from old Miss Cornelia Harborough. She distrusted strangers even more than the others did, and led a life that made a hermit seem sociable. It was a long time before I realised she even lived on my beat. Her home was in the hamlet of Waindale, and I must have walked past it countless times without realising the place was inhabited. It was a tumbledown cottage, more of a ruin than the genuine ruins in the area. The upper windows were hanging from their frames, the front door was always open and the place bore an air of total neglect. The garden was overgrown and the path to the front door was merely a foot-trod through the tall, lanky growth of mixed weeds. The house next door to Miss Harborough's was derelict and the two dwellings resembled those drawings of ghostly ruins which appear frequently in Victorian topographical works.

My first meeting with Miss Harborough came when I was standing outside the telephone kiosk in Waindale one summer's afternoon, some six weeks after my arrival. It was a glorious day and I was basking in the warmth, clad in full uniform because I was on motor-cycle patrol. I became aware of a tiny old lady inching nervously across the road towards me. She wore a quaint little hat made of purple raffia with a huge flower in the front, and she sported a flowered pinny over a long, black dress. She looked like something out of a Dickens novel as she edged closer to me. Her face was elfin-like, pinched and wizened, but her teeth were beautiful. She must have been well over seventy.

"Are you the policeman?" she came very close before asking the question.

"I am," I tried to sound pleasant.

"There is a little matter I wish to discuss with you," she said solemnly.

"Can we talk here?" I suggested, wondering if she would step onto the footpath where I waited near the telephone kiosk for the call that may or may not come.

"It's very confidential," she spoke grimly. "Can you come into my house?"

"Certainly," I said. "Where do you live?"

"Over there, at Corner Cottage," and she pointed to the hovel.

"There?" I must have sounded horrified.

"Yes, over there. Come over, will you, when your call comes through," and off she paddled. I watched her negotiate the empty road and weave through the long grass towards her gaping front door. She squeezed through the gap and vanished inside. I waited at the telephone kiosk for my statutory five minutes in case I was needed by the sergeant, but no calls came. I was free to socialise with Miss Harborough. I crossed the road, plodded along the grassy path and reached her front door. It would not open any further, nor would it close. It hung from its hinges, rotten and slimy, so I squeezed through and found myself in a very dark living-room. The rear window was completely covered with greenery on the outside, utterly overgrown with rampant vegetation and the whole place reeked of dampness. The room was so full of furniture that some of it was piled on chairs and tables, and there was barely any space to squeeze between the items. Everything was Victorian, and was probably worth a fortune in a sale-room. Its condition here left a lot to be desired. Much of it was rotting and broken – it was such a pity. Then she appeared.

To this day, I do not know where she had been, nor do I know where she ate, slept or sat. The room was so full of furniture that it obscured all doorways other than the one I had used, and she appeared to pop from behind a pile of chairs. Perhaps she maintained a tunnel into a back room?

I had never seen the old thing before this day. I had never seen a vehicle call at the house to sell bread, meat or fruit, and there was no shop in this little hamlet. Buses never passed this way and she had no transport, not even a cycle. Her lights did not work and I guessed there was no toilet. I saw no taps either. But here she lived and, later, when I tried to interest the social services in her, she refused to leave. She could not be forcibly removed because she was not insane, nor was she a burden on the State, or a nuisance to anyone. I later tried to mend her door and to effect a repair upon her electrical system, but she would not hear of it. She was the epitome of independence. Stubborn, perhaps, but fascinating. How she managed to survive remains a mystery to me.

But her reason for calling me into her cottage that day was, in her mind, very urgent and very confidential.

"What do you want?" I asked.

"I have found this," and from the pocket of her pinny, she produced a sixpence. Today, in decimalised currency, it is worth $2\frac{1}{2}$ pence.

"Where?"

"Outside my house, in the gutter," she told me.

When dealing with found property, the police must be extremely careful. A policeman who accepts property from a member of the public must always make a detailed entry in his notebook, give a receipt to the finder and ensure that the incident is fully recorded in his official notebook and in records at the police station. He must not forget to hand in the property at the end of his shift, otherwise he could be accused of stealing it. With items of no particular value or importance, like cash in small amounts, it is customary to let the finder keep the article and merely make a record of the finding, should the loser make a claim. The loser will then be referred to the finder. If property is unclaimed within a certain time, in our case three months, the finder may retain it and regard it as his own, always remembering that the loser has a claim of title to it.

It was my intention to deal with Miss Harborough's sixpence in that manner. I would tell her to keep it and if it was not claimed within three months, it would be hers. The chances of anyone reporting its loss were remote, to say the least.

"I'll make a note of it," I told her, but in reality I had no intention of noting this. No one would come seeking a lost sixpence and so far as I was concerned, she could keep it. I made a note of her name and address, and the fact she had found it three weeks ago. I said, "Keep it, Miss Harborough. If it is not claimed within three months, it is yours to keep."

"Oh, no," she insisted. "You must take it and you must make enquiries to find the loser. That is your duty, is it not?

Someone will have lost this coin and may be looking for it. Someone, may be, who cannot afford to lose money like this. That is why I called you in, to do your duty."

Inwardly, I groaned. If I took this to the office, the sergeant would half kill me. There would have to be entries in all manner of official places, a receipt would have to be issued, I would have to drive out here with the receipt for her and then, if it wasn't claimed within three months, the superintendent would have to write to Miss Harborough to ask if she wanted to claim the coin. I would have to motor down to Malton to collect it, against signature, and then drive out here to deliver it, against her signature, a round trip of thirty-three miles. Was a sixpence worth that?

"No, Miss Harborough, please. You must retain it." I tried to be firm. "I will make a record in our official books, and if the loser has reported the loss, we will send him along to you."

"No, officer, I insist. I do not want it in the house. It is your duty to accept the coin and to make enquiries to trace the loser."

Such tasks were not part of our duty, but she wasn't to know that. It seems I had no choice. I accepted the coin and was then compelled to go through the motions of recording it in our official system, much to the chagrin, and I suspect, amusement of Sergeant Blaketon. Three months later, I had to return to Miss Harborough because the coin had not been claimed. Even then, she refused to accept it. She wanted nothing to do with it, because it was not hers. I told her I would donate it to a police charity, and she agreed. The Widows and Orphans Fund derived a little benefit from her honesty.

My next contact with Miss Harborough was some time later, on the occasion of a forthcoming Government Census. She had received forms to complete and wanted help. She called me in and had the forms spread across a table. When she explained she wanted help to fill them in, I said, "Fine, let's do it now."

"Oh, no. You can't do that," she cried. "It asks for details of persons living in this house at midnight. It's only three o'clock in the afternoon now."

"That doesn't matter," I tried to convince her. "You know who'll be here at midnight. There's only you."

"You might be here," she corrected me. "You will come to help me, won't you? It definitely says midnight . . . ."

"I can't come," I had to duck out of this one. "I've my own forms to fill in, you see, at midnight. I'll have to be at my own house, with my wife and children."

She looked a little sad but accepted the logic of my argument. She was happier than she had been a few minutes earlier, for I explained how to complete the paperwork. I later discovered, however, that she had called in a local farmer, asking him to fill in her forms at midnight. Knowing her well, he had obliged, and had sat in her house until the clock struck twelve. He had even put his name on her form, just to keep her happy.

I often wonder what the census officials made of that.

*   *   *   *

Another character with whom I made an early contact was a small scruffy individual of indeterminate age who went by the name of Aud George. No one used his surname and I learned eventually that he had retired from a life of farm labouring to live alone in a cottage at the edge of Aidensfield. I reckoned he must be about seventy, although he could have been anywhere between fifty and eighty, judging by his appearance and demeanour. He habitually wore black hob-nailed boots, gaiters, corduroy trousers and an old rough shirt without a collar, albeit with a collar stud eternally in position at the neck. His jacket was fashioned from something resembling Harris tweed and it must have seen the passage of many years. He wore a cap, even when getting washed, and spent his days wandering up and down the village street, chatting to anyone who could spare the time. Aud George was a fixture in that street.

The prefix *Aud* is an old North Riding term of affection. Strictly interpreted, it means *old,* but it is seldom used in that sense. Way back in the seventeenth and eighteenth centuries, when witches were said to roam those moors, old women suspected of witchcraft were known by this prefix – Aud Nan, Aud Annie, Aud Meg and Aud Sue were examples. Even today, tales linger about Aud Nanny of Stokesley, Aud Nan of Spittal Houses, Aud Mother Stebbins and many more. The devil himself was known as "T'Aud 'Un" (The Old One), but in recent times, the term Aud has come to mean something approaching affection, possibly tinged with respect. Young boys in my schooldays would call one another Aud Bernard, Aud Alf, Aud Bill, Aud Fred, etc., as a term of affection or friendship, and the practice has endured over the years. The term is still heard in the moorland villages.

It was quite normal, therefore, that George should be known by this prefix and everyone knew him by that name. The story goes that a stranger arrived at Aidensfield seeking a Mr Clotherstone, but the man had not been furnished with Clotherstone's address. He had found Aud George in his usual position on the seat in front of the church and asked where Mr Clotherstone lived.

"Nay," George had said. "Ah dissn't know onnybody of that name."

"He definitely lives here," the man had insisted. "I'm from Adamson and Smythe, solicitors, and I must see him. I have made enquiries and have traced him to this village. He is known to live here."

George had shaken his head. "Nay, lad, thoo's foxed me. There's neearbody called that in Aidensfield."

"He used to work on a farm, I'm told," the man persisted, "and his first name was George."

"George?" asked Aud George. "Thoo dissn't mean Aud George, doest tha?"

"Yes," beamed the man. "That's what I was told. Ask for Aud George."

"Then that's me!" George had thrust out his chest. "I'm Aud George, so that must make me Mr Clotherstone, eh?"

And so he was.

Because of our respective regular use of that street, my contact with Aud George was frequent and invariably interesting. He was a fund of information, a veritable village knowledge-box. Such a person is of inestimable value to a policeman, even if much of his chatter is pure gossip. George would chatter away quite amiably, giving me titbits of information which were useful to me in my work and which he knew would be of value. He did not do so with any malice in his mind, nor did he bear a grudge against anyone. He provided me with snippets simply because I ought to know what was going on. He would tell me, for example, that young Stan Fowler had taken up the hobby of throwing stones through greenhouse windows, or that Andy Merryweather's daughter was seeing rather a lot of a married man, or that Charlie Brett's lad was riding a motor-bike without a licence, or that young Ferrensby, aged seventeen, was supping ale in a local pub.

These snippets were of value, as was any other gossip, but occasionally he did provide very useful information. He had once noticed a car pass through Aidensfield at a slow speed, noted the number on the back of his hand, and then told me. It transpired that it was a team of confidence tricksters from Leeds who preyed on the elderly by offering to repair roofs or windows. Having done the work, which was shoddy in the extreme, they demanded exorbitant prices for the job, against veiled threats of violence if they refused to pay. This information was valuable and in fact, a colleague of mine on another beat arrested that bunch due to George's observations. They were awarded three years apiece for their crimes.

With regard to George's minor gems of news, I seldom took official action. For example, it was sufficient to stop Charlie Brett's lad and tell him I'd be checking his driving licence in a day or two, or I would pop into the pub to inform the landlord that young Ferrensby was under age. I maintained that this form of prevention was often better than taking the offenders to court, although such actions could be construed as being over-generous in the exercise of my traditional discretion. The ability to use such discretion is under attack by left-wing political elements who see it as favouritism and something to be enjoyed by privileged classes. Nothing could be further from the truth, for those helped in this manner are usually the modern under-privileged who, without this assistance from the police, would soon acquire a criminal record. Keen socialists are attempting to remove that valuable exercise of discretion from the policeman's armoury – it will be a sad day when it has gone. When it does go, the feared police state will have arrived when all rules will be obeyed, down to the last cruel letter of the law. Human policemen will no longer exist.

But back to George. My many talks with him revealed one charming habit which I don't think he realised he possessed. It concerned the passing of information about local deaths.

George would keep everyone, including me, informed about the latest deaths in Aidensfield and district. At first, the names he provided meant nothing to me, but after I had been in the area for a few months, they did begin to have relevance. I could associate names with houses, houses with faces and faces with the inevitable range of close relatives who lived hereabouts. Consequently, a death was important. It meant I could commiserate with the relatives of the deceased, should I chance to meet them in the street, and that sort of interest in other folks is useful Public Relations for any police officer.

After a while, I realised that George was unwittingly using a code when he passed on this information. He employed different phrases which were based on the religion of the dear departed, consequently it was possible to identify the religion of the deceased from the words used by George.

If a member of the Church of England died, for example, he would say, "He's seen t'last of his days," and for a Roman Catholic, he would gravely tell me, "He's gitten his time owered." For a Methodist, he would say, "He's gone to better things," and for members of the smaller churches, his phrase would be, "He's drawn his last."

Inevitably, there were those who professed no specific faith, but who would be placed to rest within the boundaries of the local parish church, officially enlisted in the great army of deceased members of the Church of England. For these, George's phrase was, "They've gone to their eternal rest, God bless 'em."

I enjoyed his chatter and we became great pals. He served the public of the district for many years and in all weathers. He was there when I left Aidensfield for pastures new, but I ought to add his own epitaph. I learned a few years ago that he had died. His own death was announced in his Anglican phrase, and I was sorry I was not there to learn of it first-hand.

I am told, however, that Aud George died slowly and very

peacefully, and that his own last words were "Ah's gahin to meet my Maker."

*   *   *   *

As I progressed around my beat in those early days, meeting people like Aud George, Miss Harborough and Farmer Bradshaw, I realised that those country folk were thoroughly decent people. They were good and they were harmless; there wasn't an ounce of evil in them. If they broke the laws of this land, then it was in a small way. They forget to renew their driving licences, got drunk on Saturday night, drove unroadworthy vehicles or let cattle stray on the highway. These are not evil transgressions like vandalism, violence and theft. Crime, in the real sense of the word was a rare part of my routine police duties. If I had to 'book' any of these people, that act of police duty was never held against me. They stoically accepted a court appearance or a fine and our friendship was never tainted. They considered errors on their part to be their fault, and knew that a constable's duty must be done. Once in a while, therefore, I was duty bound to take one of my 'parishioners' to court.

Such an occasion involved a local character called Dick the Sick. A dour Scotsman, he loved a practical joke and could be talked into all manner of japes after a pint or two of strong Yorkshire ale. Once a joke misfired because it involved the police in an official way.

I was on my weekly rest-day at the time, and the incident involved a famous greyhound which had been stolen. The Press was full of the story but it transpired that George, landlord of the Hopbind Inn at Elsinby, bred greyhounds. He used them in the popular sport of coursing and it was unfortunate that he had recently banned Dick from his bars, due to previous pranks. Dick had acquired his nickname of "Dick the Sick" because he never worked, always managing to exist on sickness benefits and other Government handouts. In spite of his multiple ailments, Dick and his wife had produced eight lovely children and a cottage garden as tidy as any for miles around.

On the occasion of the theft of the greyhound, someone

anonymously rang the nearest Divisional Police Headquarters to say the dog in question had been hidden at the Hopbind Inn, Elsinby.

As a result of information received, as we say in police jargon, a police car proceeded from that Headquarters with an inspector, a sergeant and two constables on board. In the jargon of newspapers, they swooped upon the unsuspecting Hopbind and its customers and mounted a very thorough search. They found many greyhounds, of course, but the stolen dog was not among them. From the ensuing conversation with the landlord, it became quite clear that the call had been a hoax. It also became clear from the distinctive Scots accent of the caller, that it had been perpetrated by Dick the Sick. George knew that, and Dick's motive wasn't difficult to imagine. Dick was interviewed by that army of officers, but he stoutly denied making the call.

Next morning, being totally unaware of this little drama on my patch, I booked on duty to find Sergeant Blaketon waiting on my doorstep. He provided me with a lurid account of the hoax call and of the alleged whereabouts of the famous missing dog. He went on to say the inspector had not been very pleased about it, and suggested we have another talk with Dick, in an attempt to secure an admission from him. We found him in his garden and when he saw the impressive bulk of Sergeant Blaketon, he wilted visibly. During the interview, however, he persistently denied responsibility for the call. I knew by his facial expressions and the way he ran his hand through his thick red hair, that he was guilty. But that sort of evidence is useless in a court of law. The more old Blaketon pressured him, the more firmly he denied our allegations. As we turned to leave, beaten by his Scots stubbornness, Dick tugged at my sleeve and said, "I'd like a word with you, Mr Rhea, please."

"Alone, Dick?"

"Aye, alone."

Blaketon gave me the nod and I went into Dick's tidy home. In the lounge, he looked at me, licked his lips and said, "It was me, Mr Rhea."

"I know it was, Dick, but why? Why make a bloody stupid call like that?"

"Aye, it was stupid. They got me tipsy, you see. They dared me to do it."

"Who did?"

"Them in the Brewer's Arms." That was a pub in Aidensfield.

"I'll have to book you, Dick," I told him and explained all about the fuss and the visits by other police officers.

"It'll get it off my chest," he sighed, and I thought I detected relief in his voice.

On his own admission, I reported him for summons and eventually he appeared at Eltering Magistrates' Court, charged with making an annoying telephone call. He was fined £5.

A few days later, I dropped into the bar of the Brewer's Arms where the place was alive with local men, still chuckling over Dick's dilemma. Dick was there, suffering them in a broody silence. As I walked in, the expected hush descended upon the assembly, as it always did when a uniformed bobby entered. Looking around the bunch of rosy, rural faces, I adopted a serious expression and said, "Well, gentlemen, Dick's been fined. Five pounds. It's not a lot, but it's a big amount for a chap with eight kids and no job. You've had your fun, all of you. I know you put him up to that joke," and I then adopted an even more serious tone. "It is an offence to aid, abet, counsel or procure the commission of an offence by any person. You're all guilty of that, each and every one of you."

They did not utter a word, but all looked at me steadily, wondering what was their fate.

"But," I continued, "I will not summon you if you do one small thing for me. I reckon you ought to contribute to Dick's fine, all of you," I had a quick count of heads and there were fifteen in the bar. "I reckon ten bob apiece would be about right, eh?"

No one moved. No one said a thing. "It could be a fiver each," I reminded them, "and your names in police files." I removed my notebook from the pocket of my tunic and opened it, as if to take names.

"We've had our fun, lads," said one farmer, as he dug into his pocket and produced some cash. "Ten bob's nowt."

He passed a ten shilling note to me and his action prompted the others into passing me a similar amount. I soon had £7 10s. 0d. (£7.50) in my hand. I passed this to Dick.

"There you are, Dick. You're in pocket and your fine's been paid."

"You'll have a drink on me, Mr Rhea?" he asked, smiling.

"Aye, I will," I said, for it's not often a Scotsman buys a Yorkshireman a drink.

But that's how the Dicks of this world exist without the need to work. Somehow, they always win.

* * * *

Another character I shall never forget is a nameless youth in a distant village. Soon after my arrival in Aidensfield, I found myself performing what we called 'routes'. In the early days of policing, these were undertaken either on foot or by pedal-cycle, and they were allocated to each rural policeman by a superior officer. Some routes were late at night and others very early in the morning, even starting at 4 am. Each route lasted about three or four hours and we had to follow a predetermined route around our area of responsibility. In the days before personal radios for policemen, we had to arrive at specified telephone kiosks at certain times, so that the office could contact us if our presence was required at an incident. The 'points', as we called them, enabled our superiors to find us and to check upon our whereabouts. Those points were used both as a method of communication and for supervisory purposes. The sergeant, the inspector or even the superintendent would get out of bed at the crack of dawn to drive out to one of our lonely points, hoping to find the duty policeman. A short conference would be held, and the superior would sign the constable's notebook to record the fact of that meeting. We nicknamed this curious little procedure as a 'chalk', probably from the days when the supervisory rank carried a little slate and chalked up the time of the meeting. If the visit was before 6 am or after midnight, the entry would be in red. It was considered quite an achievement to acquire two or three red chalks during a month.

The arrival of radio-equipped police motor-cycles suggested that this ancient and mainly useless activity could be dispensed with. But it wasn't. Old habits die hard and we had to drive around those routes on our motor-cycles, continuing to make points at telephone kiosks. This was insisted upon, even though we had radio sets. Although modern equipment was coming to the police, modern ideas were a long way behind. I am reminded of a sergeant at a local station who, upon receiving the first consignment of personal radio sets worth around £100 each, refused to let the men use them. "They're too valuable for you lads to mess about with," he said, locking them in a cupboard.

As a result of this rigid thinking, therefore, I regularly found myself motor-cycling about my beat either at the crack of dawn or during the depths of night. The sound of the little Francis Barnett two-stroke must have woken the populace, caused dogs to bark, cattle to low and hens to cackle. Little else was achieved by these patrols, simply because any self-respecting burglar or poacher would hear the distinctive sound of the bike long before the constabulary hove to. But authority said we had to perform them, and so we did. I often thought they were designed for supervisory officers to acquire lots of red chalks, like a gunman of the wild west notching up kills on his rifle butt. I wondered if some of our supervisors ran competitions to see who could acquire the most red chalks within a given time, with a prize at the end of the year. Like a length of red chalk, maybe?

One evening, I performed a late route, working from 7 pm until 11 pm, and then the following morning, I was allocated another one beginning at 6 am. This was before the days when we could demand eight hours off duty between shifts, and so, at six o'clock that morning, I leapt aboard my little Francis Barnett, kicked it into life and began a long, cold and dark tour of lonely moorland and twisting lanes. This particular route took me away from Aidensfield because a neighbouring bobby was on leave. I had to cover his beat.

I was rather concerned because my petrol was low. Because I had to obtain my official petrol from a specified local garage, I could not purchase any elsewhere; besides, garages weren't open at that early hour. I knew I would have to be careful, at least until eight-thirty when my local garage was able to supply me.

At my seven o'clock point, I received a phone call asking me to deliver a 'request message'. It meant a long detour to a lonely farm – it was to inform a farmer that Uncle Frank had died in Middlesbrough General Hospital and would he contact the sister on Ward 9. Having delivered this message (a task we often had to undertake before the increasing popularity of telephones in these remote places), I returned to my route, noting that my eight o'clock point was the hamlet of Whemmelby, at the telephone kiosk.

Whemmelby lies deep in the North Yorkshire moors at the top of a long glacial valley etched deep into the hills. In the spring-time, it is glorious with daffodils and bluebells which coat its nine miles of riverside, and in the autumn, the moors above glow with a rich, deep purple. It is a robust area, with long and low farm houses built snug into the hillsides. Its centre of population is a cluster of houses at the foot of a hill with a gradient of 1-in-3. There are several hills of this gradient in the North Yorkshire moors, and while they hold no terrors for the locals who use them daily, they do terrify town drivers and others from the flat regions of Britain who regard 1-in-12 as precipitous.

It was down one of these hills that I guided my Francis Barnett to make that eight o'clock point. Half way down, the engine stopped. I knew immediately what had happened, so I coasted into the hamlet and pulled up outside the kiosk. I inspected my petrol tank and, sure enough, it was bone dry. My fears had been confirmed and I was seventeen miles from my usual garage.

My radio would not function because of my location deep in the valley, so I went into the kiosk to ring Divisional Headquarters. I hoped they might arrange a car to fetch some petrol, but the phone was out of order. There was a small notice stuck to a window pane, but I tried the instrument just in case it had been repaired at the exchange end. It hadn't. It was stone dead.

What now? I knew Whemmelby from the past, and there was nothing here, not even a shop. There was a village hall with a small parking area in front, Methodist chapel, three farms and one or two cottages, all surrounded by steep hills and forbidding moorland. I looked at each building in the hope of seeing a tell-tale telephone cable running to it, but not one of them possessed a telephone. I could not push the bike up that incline and the nearest garage would be about eight miles away. I couldn't obtain my official petrol there, but I might be able to buy some at my own expense, hopefully just enough to get me home.

Another problem was the performance of my duty. Suppose that phone accepted incoming calls? Suppose Sergeant Blaketon rang me and instructed me to visit some house which had been burgled, or to attend a traffic accident or other calamity? I dreaded to think what his reaction might be when I said I'd run out of petrol, and I concluded that the only solution was to walk up the hill in the hope that a friendly motorist picked me up and transported me to a petrol filling station.

That course of action meant parking the machine in a safe place, not that anyone here would harm it but because Sergeant Blaketon might accuse me of carelessness with county property. I returned to the bike, sat astride it and began to propel it with my feet towards a parking place in front of the village hall.

It was then that I heard an approaching vehicle. As I manoeuvred my lifeless noddy bike across the narrow road, a tractor and trailer appeared from behind a farm house and moved towards me. It was driven by a roughly dressed youngster with long, straggly hair and a cheeky grin on his face. A large, square five-gallon can stood alone in the centre of the trailer. He stopped the tractor, jumped down from it and came over to me.

"What's up?" he asked with a friendly smile.

"Petrol," I said, feeling very foolish. "My bike's run out of petrol."

He looked at my crash helmet with POLICE across the front, examined the Francis Barnett with its radio set where the pillion should be, and peered at my uniform numerals.

"Thoo's nut our local chap?" he said by way of a question.

"No, he's on leave. I was working late last night, and I had to come out here early . . . "

"Thoo'll be wanting some juice then?" He didn't wait to hear my tale of sorrow and despair.

"I was going to walk up to Brantsford . . ."

"Neea need," he said, leaping onto the trailer. "Thoo can 'ave some of this," and he lifted the big can down. "Tak thy filler cap off."

"It needs two-stroke mixture," I said.

"This is two-stroke. Cap."

I obeyed, removing the cap from the petrol tank; he did likewise with the large red can and began to pour the precious stuff into my machine.

"Whoa!" I called. "That'll do. I just need enough to get me to a garage."

"I'll fill her up," he laughed. "Two-gallon tank, eh?"

"Yes, but there's no need . . ."

"This 'un's full, mister," and he kept on pouring. He filled my tank almost to overflowing, smiled and said, "There. That'll see thoo all right for a mile or two."

"I'll pay," I offered, starting to unbutton my motor-cycle gear. It took a long time to reach my wallet, tucked inside my inner tunic, but in the meantime, the cheerful lad had returned the can to the trailer and was sitting on the tractor seat, ready to move off.

"How much?" I shouted, still fiddling with buttons and press-studs.

"Nowt," he called back. "Thoo can have it for nowt. It's not mine, anyway."

"Not yours?" I cried, but he was moving away. I had a tank full of petrol, so I gave chase but he simply waved me away and shouted above the noise of our engines. "Have it on us, mister." He turned into a farm yard, leapt from the tractor and vanished indoors, waving me on.

I do not know who he was and I never saw him again. It was months before I made a return visit to Whemmelby, and I asked after him, but no one seemed to know who I was talking about. I never did know the true owner of that petrol.

But my petrol problems were far from over. Every month, we had to complete a mileage return which showed the places we had visited, the mileage covered and the petrol consumed. The return would be rigidly checked, as indeed it was, because of the milometer readings and the garage accounts. This system meant I could not show the extra two gallons on my return, for it was not part of the official intake. But my mileage had to be shown correctly – the milometer ensured that.

The result was that my motor-cycle that month registered a somewhat staggering petrol consumption, having apparently covered over 100 miles to the gallon instead of the usual 80. I pleaded total ignorance for the cause of this astounding feat of motoring and swore blind that I had never coasted down-hill in my own economy drive. The next thing that happened was that my machine was taken to Headquarters for a thorough check by the county mechanics, and the garage from whom I purchased my official petrol was asked to carefully check its accounts. There were no discrepancies. Officially, my motor-cycle had done remarkably well that month, and all supervisory officers showed great interest in its next performance. I had to disappoint them, because things returned to normal.

Later, when I had time to reflect upon the incident, I did wonder if a friendly farmer had sent that life-saving can on the trailer. Was it coincidence that a tractor and trailer carrying a five-gallon can of two-stroke fuel arrived just in time to save me from a long, perspiring walk? Or had it been neatly arranged by a friendly farmer who had witnessed my dilemma from his breakfast table?

I shall never know, but if he reads this he will know that I was truly thankful, even if the police garage manager did grow a little more grey around the gills due to the strange behaviour of the Aidensfield motor-cycle. If that manager reads this, *he'll* know what happened too!

Three

The existence of the Slemmington Hunt was revealed to me shortly before eleven o'clock one morning. I had been on half-nights the previous day, i.e. working from 6 pm until 2 am, and had climbed from my lovely bed at ten o'clock. I had staggered bleary-eyed into the kitchen to find Mary had taken the car and the children, and had gone shopping in Ashfordly. I was alone, and it was time for breakfast.

After hunting in vain for the milk to add to my cornflakes, I realised it had probably just arrived and went outside to seek it. As I lifted the three creamy-tops from their resting place on the front doorstep, there was a thundering of mighty hooves accompanied by a deafening jangle of harness very close to me. I was rather surprised to see a massive horse leap across my garden fence. It galloped across the lawn and vanished over my far railings in a fog of minute pieces of flying earth, leaving my lawn like a recently used tank route. Sitting astride the animal was a man wearing a black riding cap, a red hunting jacket (called pink) and white jodhpurs and he shouted, "Tally-Ho" or something vaguely similar. Then silence descended.

I was not sure whether this was really happening and as I gazed after that apparition in an attempt to determine 'yes' or 'no', untold numbers of similar creatures accompanied by baying dogs, leapt the railings at the east of my garden, shouted in strange voices and vanished over the fence at the other side. They hooted and galloped down the hill into Aidensfield to disappear for ever from my sight. Straggling hounds followed, baying and sniffing, and one of them looked at me with baleful eyes, thought the better of it and ran to join his pals.

It probably took a mere second or two for this incident to

41

act itself out, but it seemed an eternity. I stood on my
doorstep, rubbing my eyes and wondering if I was in the
middle of a dream about the Valkyries but the battered
surface of my lawn bore evidence of genuine horses. The place
was riddled with hoof marks. A multitude of tiny sods littered
the place, rather like the main track at York Racecourse after
the Ebor Handicap is over. It had happened all right. I was
too tired and amazed to be angry; I simply stood and gaped
at the holes, all neatly shaped like horse-shoes.

It occurred to me, quite suddenly, that the fox might be
somewhere in my house. The front door was open, but I
didn't think it had darted between my legs. The garage doors
were open too, and so was the side door into the passage. I
hastily closed the front door, deposited the milk bottles and
made a hurried search of my premises. I saw nothing of a fox.
The hunt did not return, so I enjoyed a comparatively peaceful breakfast, wondering if this sort of thing was a regular
occurrence.

Perhaps one of the most mysterious aspects of the hunting
set is their ability to make strange noises via the mouth. Their
'yoiks' and 'tally-hos' carry a tone of unreality and some of
their yodelling is impossible to copy or impersonate with any
degree of authenticity. It seems that the ability to yodel is
something bred into that class of person, something which he
emits only when on horseback and only when the hounds are
milling around. Sometimes, as I sat in my kitchen listening to
them in the distance, I wondered if huntsmen practised their
calls. To be as proficient as that on a cold and frosty morning
must take years of practice and hours of devoted throat-
warbling. I believe Peter Ustinov had great difficulty
emulating the sound when filming "Lady L" at nearby Castle
Howard. He tried in vain to yodel like a North Yorkshire
huntsman and even though he was coached by some first-class
exponents in the art, the true sound eluded him. He spent
many an hour walking around the estate in full cry, and I
often wonder what the locals thought about him. For that
matter, I wonder what the foxes thought about him.

Be that as it may, those who participate in such pastimes
are a race apart. True huntsmen are born, not made. Robert
Smith Surtees in his *Handley Cross* sums it up by writing:

" 'Unting fills my thoughts by day and many a good run I
have in my sleep. No man is fit to be called a sportsman wot
doesn't kick his wife out of bed on a haverage once in three
weeks." Although I had been born and bred in the fox-
hunting and otter-hunting territory of the North Riding
moorland, I never took part in any of those sports. Other
than attempting to follow a hunt on foot, my only involvement in such matters was a shooting trip with my
grandfather. It was during one of the annual February
pigeon-shoots. Armed with a .410 shotgun, and aged only
sixteen, I tramped the hills with him, shooting at hundreds
of pigeons and hitting none. I don't think I was capable of
hitting them, not because I was a bad shot – I wasn't – but
somehow my love of birds and animals caused my aim to
wander. My only hint of success came when I shot at an
unsuspecting pigeon which was about to land on a distant
tree. I released both barrels and the only result was the angry
appearance of a man who had been sheltering beneath that
very tree. In his moments of solitude, he had been showered
with falling twigs and spent lead shot, but escaped with his
life. So did the pigeon.

I was to learn that fox-hunting is almost a religion in
Aidensfield and district. Because of the damage to my lawn, I
made enquiries around the village in an attempt to establish
my legal rights. I was told, quite politely, that the local hunt
had the right to cross and re-cross my land, and indeed lots of
other land in the locality. I failed to find anything to state
otherwise and it seemed that this was one of those grey areas
of law where no hard-and-fast rule existed. It had been
happening for generations, and probably would continue to
happen until the socialists banned the sport.

Thankfully, the hunters hadn't leapt into the lower part of
the garden where it was thick with equipment and children's
toys. I did wonder what would have happened if one of the
horses got its head fast in the children's swing or put a foot
through a cloche. It seemed I had to allow them access to my
lawn. But after that occasion, they never leapt my way again.
One of the reasons may have been that whenever I learned
they were hunting in our area, I parked my car outside my
garage, right in the path of any horse that might leap my

garden fence. If a horse landed on that, it would be another insurance job.

That single brush with the hunt was my only personal complaint against them. I spoke to the Master of Fox Hounds about it, and he was polite but firm in his right to hunt across land in the vicinity. Like many other people, whether from town or country, I found the sight of the meet very thrilling. At times, there were as many as 25 pairs of hounds, 200 horsemen and upwards of 100 foot followers meeting in the grounds of the great houses of the district. The spectacle was fascinating, all colour and excitement, and the party would enjoy the traditional stirrup-cup before setting off in pursuit of old Reynard the cunning. It was a fine sight and one of the essential parts of the English countryside.

Whether or not one agrees with the hunting of foxes, the sight of a hunt in full cry is guaranteed to thrill. The cunning of the fox, the skill of the hounds and the uncanny knowledge of the hunters, all combine to make the day memorable for everyone. A kill is seldom of any great importance – the fun, they say, lies in the chase.

For centuries in these hills, men have pitted their wits against the fox. Today, there seem to be just as many foxes; it has been said that hunting them destroys the weaklings and therefore breeds a strong strain thus proving the adage 'only the strong survive'. The foxes are experts too – they win by 'going to ground', as otters 'go to couch'; some foxes are tempted by the skills of foot hunters too. For example, some foresters spotted a fox making towards them. They were down-wind of him, beyond his range of scent, so they tried to coax him into coming nearer. They did this by taking a blade of grass, placing it between the fingers and thumbs and blowing gently to make a whistling noise. Children often do this. The fox pricked up his ears at the sound. Was it a screaming rabbit? Something else he should investigate? But he was not fooled; he lowered his head and vanished into the undergrowth. Minutes later, the hunters arrived with their hounds, but he had gone.

On balance, I am not offended by either hunts or hunters,

and I have no personal grudge against foxes. They don't carve up my lawn.

*   *   *   *

Fox-hunting was just one of the rural sports practised on my beat. The others included coursing, fishing, shooting, gliding, hiking, football, cricket, billiards and table-tennis. There were probably others. I frequently questioned the meaning of "sport" in this context – high bred rurals consider 'sport' includes blood sports, i.e. hunting, shooting and fishing, whereas others of more lowly origins think of football, cricket, dominoes and school sports days. I suppose I could add bare-fist pugilistics, bear-baiting and public executions. The list is virtually endless.

The point is that I, as the village bobby, had to know what was happening upon my beat. As I lived and worked in a lush green part of the countryside, full of large country estates, it was sensible to familiarise myself with the sporting events occurring about me.

Sergeant Blaketon frequently quizzed me about rural affairs of this nature, for the subject seemed to fascinate him. He had spent much of his police career on the industrial fringes of Teesside, where they bred racing pigeons and grew leeks, consequently our type of sport intrigued him. I could always answer his queries and this appeared to satisfy his curiosity, although I never did learn his true opinions on sport and the gentry. I suspect the truth was that he considered himself aloof from such matters. He enforced the law – he did not hold opinions. With a head of thick black hair, thick black eyebrows and a figure like a prize fighter, he was an impressive sight. Furthermore, he was honest, straight and completely trustworthy. But he was unbending, I was to learn. He disliked his men exercising what he termed 'loose discretion'. I learned he was rigid with the public too – there were no 'warnings' from Oscar Blaketon. If someone offended against the law, he booked them. The painful decision whether or not to prosecute offenders was therefore avoided by him, and his technique ensured that the problem rested with someone higher up the promotion ladder. That's what promoted people were paid for.

For example, if he found a motorist parked without lights, he booked him. If he saw a drunk, he arrested him. If he stopped a motor-vehicle, he checked every document it carried. Some of us weren't as keen as that – we would switch on the lights of parked cars, we would put drunks into a taxi and send them home, and we would give friendly advice to those who erred slightly. Oscar might adopt our rural ways in time, we felt, for I learned he had arrived at Ashfordly only weeks before I came to Aidensfield. We were both new to the locality.

Knowing of his rigid attitude, I wondered why he allowed Alwyn's chrysanthemums to flourish in the female cell. I learned, by way of an answer, that Sergeant Blaketon hated gardening; if Alwyn was not permitted to use the cell, his glorious display would have to occupy a prominent position in the garden next door to Blaketon's house. Blaketon must have realised that his wife would react violently to such a gorgeous floral display so close to her kitchen window, and he was happy that she never set eyes on it. It seemed he was content never to examine the female cell. No one saw him enter it. Knowing Blaketon, however, I knew that procedure would have been among his priorities upon arrival here. He'd obviously opened the door, seen the blooms and made a very rapid decision. He was a man with a fast-moving brain, I decided.

It was his attention to detail and his rigid adherence to the rules, that caused me to think twice when George Ward, landlord of the Hopbind Inn, Elsinby, asked if he could run greyhound races in a local field.

My initial reaction was to wonder why he had asked me and to say, "Go ahead", but the figure of Oscar Blaketon loomed uneasily in the background. We sometimes called him "Occurrence Book" because of his initials; this was an essential document at police stations, a record of every incident that happened, and it was known as the "O.B.". My knowledge of O.B.'s adherence to rules halted me.

"I'll let you know," I told George. "When do you want to run them?"

"Friday nights," he said. "We were thinking of having half a dozen races or so, around Harold's field down Ploatby

Lane. Starting at seven-thirty, I reckon, and finishing about half nine. One race every twenty minutes, give or take a minute or two."

"How many competitors?"

"Dunno," he shrugged his shoulders. "I've a lot of runners, and if we advertised it we'd get loads in from all over."

"A big affair, then?" I suggested.

"Oh, aye. We'd have traps and a proper track, you know. Electric hare and all that. Bookies too."

"Not just a bit of village fun, then?" I put to him.

"Not really. There is a demand for this, you know," he spoke seriously. "I've asked among my mates."

"The cars?" I asked. "Where would you park them?"

"In Harold's field. It's big enough to take a circular track, and there's room for a hundred cars."

"Noise?" I tried to anticipate the reaction of the village to this proposal.

"No problem," he assured me. "The field is nearly a mile out of Elsinby."

"It seems O.K. to me, George, but I'll check with the sergeant and let you know. When do you hope to start?"

"Three weeks on Friday."

I relayed all this information to Sergeant Blaketon and he frowned heavily. "Greyhound racing at Elsinby?" He rubbed his chin. "It can't be legal."

"Why not, Sergeant?" I asked in all innocence.

"Dunno," he admitted. "But it doesn't sound legal, does it? It's not in a proper stadium for a start."

"I can't see why a bunch of men can't race their dogs around a field," I put to him.

He shook his big black head. "It's never been done before," he said. "If it had been legal, somebody else would have thought of it."

"Maybe they have, Sergeant, maybe the big greyhound stadiums all began like this? They must have started in a small way."

"No, son, I can't accept that. They're in cities with big money behind them, they're big business right from the start. They don't begin in little ways, don't big business stadiums."

"This is just a bit of fun."

"No, son. There's summat funny here. They're up to summat."

I couldn't see what was bothering him. I went home and read my lawbooks but found nothing to disqualify those dog-lovers from racing their animals around Harold's field. Half an hour after I'd begun my studies, the phone rang.

"Sergeant Blaketon," said the voice. "Did you say they're having bookies?"

"That was the intention, Sergeant. They want to have bookies, just like a proper racetrack. There'll be hot-dog stalls, ice-cream and soup."

"They can't," he said triumphantly. "They can't have bookmakers. It's not an approved course."

I didn't answer for a moment or two. Without bookies, what fun would there be? That was the whole idea – the men and their ladies would proceed to Harold's field, place their bets on the few races and then adjourn to George's pub to drown their sorrows or to spend their winnings. Without bookmakers on the track, the whole idea was a non-starter.

"Are you there, Rhea?" I heard him call.

"Yes, Sergeant. I was just wondering if there was a way round it."

"A way round it? Our job is to adminster the law, not to find ways round it. No bookies. That's final. Tell them they can hold their meeting if they like, but without bookmakers. There must be no obstruction of the road outside the track, no noise and no trouble of any kind."

And having made that decision, he replaced the telephone. Sitting at my desk, I wondered if he was secretly smiling with immense satisfaction. I could almost see the smirk of inverted pleasure on his face. I felt sorry for George and his pals, for the notion seemed a good one. I lifted my phone and was dialling George's number at the Hopbind Inn when I recalled a visit to a donkey derby. There had been bookies there, and it had been held in a field. And it certainly wasn't an approved racetrack. If they could have bookies, why couldn't George?

I replaced the telephone and lifted my battered copy of *Moriarty's Police Law* from its shelf and began to examine it. There was a good deal of information about approved race-tracks and I learned that a 'dog race' meant "A race in which an object propelled by mechanical means is pursued by dogs." That was contained in section 20 of the Betting and Lotteries Act of 1934, then in force. A 'track' meant premises on which races of any description, athletic sports or other sporting events took place.

There was a lot of information about the procedures required to secure licences to authorise betting on tracks. I learned, however, that special rules appertained to dog tracks. For example, betting could not take place in connection with more than eight dog races and was restricted to one continuous period not exceeding four hours. George's proposal seemed to comply with this provision. I discovered that the Totalisator could be set up on a dog track on any appointed day while the public were admitted and it could be operated for persons resorting to the track, on dog races run on that track on that day.

All this appeared to be running in George's favour and I even learned that bookmakers could not be excluded from a track being lawfully run, and that space for bookmaking should be afforded them. But all this applied to "approved" racetracks. It seemed that the local councils were empowered to grant licences for racetracks and to authorise betting on them, provided two months' prior notice was given.

I began to accept the superior knowledge of Sergeant Blaketon. His long experience was his salvation. He knew what could or could not occur. George couldn't function with bookies! And then I found the salvation clause!

I learned that bookmaking could not be carried on on *any* track unless the occupier held a licence in force under the provisions of the Betting and Lotteries Act 1934, authorising betting facilities on that track. And I discovered that the prohibition did not apply to any track on which bookmaking had not been carried out on more than seven previous days in that year, beginning on July 1, provided seven days' postal notice of the intended bookmaking had been given to the chief officer of police by the occupier.

So there it was. Long-winded, but there in print. George would be the 'occupier' of the field for this purpose, and all he had to do was give written notice to the chief constable. This did not even amount to a request for permission. It was simply a notification of the event, so I rang George. I explained this to him and told him that he could hold no more than seven days racing in any year, starting each July, and that bookies could come and accept bets on the field. He was delighted.

Sergeant Blaketon did not express his feelings when I acquainted him with this piece of legislation. He simply said, "Oh, yes?" and put down the telephone.

I was off duty on the night of the first meeting in Harold's field and went along in my civilian clothes to enjoy an unusual evening's entertainment. As I entered the field, George waved me across for a chat.

"Nice gathering, Mr Rhea," he beamed his appreciation and gazed around the chattering crowd. The place was almost full and even on this small field, there was the unmistakable atmosphere of a racecourse. Bookies were calling the odds, people were talking shop and discussing the runners, a hot-dog stall was making a fortune and the car-parking fees would keep Harold happy – whoever Harold was.

"Have you many runners, George?" I asked, walking into the centre with him.

"Full house," he told me. "Thirty in all. Some good dogs among 'em too. Six races, five to a race. Having a bet, are you?"

"I'm not much of a betting man," I said, truthfully.

"Put ten bob on No. 3 in the fourth," he advised, winking at me. "My way of saying thanks. I rang your office some weeks ago, you know, before I spoke to you. They said I couldn't have bookies. I know you found I could and I appreciate that."

"It's all part of the service, George."

"Don't forget then, No. 3."

I left him to go about his duties and went to one of the bookies' stands where I learned that No. 3 in the fourth race was called Rob Roy. I put ten shillings each way on him and settled to watch the intervening races. Just before the start of the fourth, I spotted Sergeant Blaketon, towering above the race-goers. I was in two minds whether or not to approach him, but decided I should. I pushed through the crowds and hailed him by waving my race sheet.

"Good evening, Sergeant," I was very formal.

"All quiet?" he asked, as if I was on duty.

"A very well behaved bunch, Sergeant. Their cars are all off the road, and there's no noise. Just good-humoured fun, all around."

"I didn't know whether you'd be here, son, seeing you're off duty."

He started to walk into the arena and I fell into step at his side.

"I came to see what goes on, Sergeant. I've never been to a thing of this kind."

"Me neither," he admitted. "Have you had a bet then?"

"Just one. I'm not a betting man," I told him.

"Which dog?"

I looked at him as we walked. I wasn't on duty, therefore I was permitted to have a bet. Was he catching me out?

"Rob Roy, Sergeant, in this race."

"Is it any good?"

"I was advised to put my cash on that one, Sergeant," I smiled. "It's the only bet I've placed."

In a flash, he had his wallet out and was waving a pound note at me. "I can't place a bet when I'm in uniform – stick a quid on for me, ten bob each way. That dog, same as yours."

I hurried to a bookmaker and managed to place his bet just before betting closed. To our delight, Rob Roy won handsomely at four to one and we were nicely in pocket.

"You know, P.C. Rhea," he was always very formal. "I could have made a nasty mistake there, couldn't I? If I'd forbidden that meeting, someone might have discovered those sections in the Betting and Lotteries Act. They could have complained to the Chief Constable, eh? I'd have been in serious trouble. I'm pleased you sorted it out – you did a good job. And you did it without twisting the law. We administered the law, which is our duty. Well done, lad," and he strode off.

"Thank you, Sergeant," and I adjourned to the Hopbind Inn where celebrations were already being held. I had the reason, and the cash, to celebrate.

* * * *

One sport which I had never seen before and which was

totally new to me, was hare coursing. I had never been in contact with it, but soon after my arrival at Aidensfield, I learned that the headquarters of the Ryedale Coursing Club was at the Brewer's Arms, Aidensfield. The pub was the headquarters of almost every other village organisation, ranging from the Catholic Women's League to the British Legion, so the identity of the Coursing Club's HQ did not surprise me. Coursing meetings were held at Aidensfield during the winter of each year.

My very first coursing meeting came one crisp November day. I was on duty at the time, which meant I could officially visit the scene; in fact, I was allocated that duty because of the expected traffic influx and other associated problems. There would be a bar, for example, and I had to be on guard against youngsters buying ale. Such is the lot of the rural policeman – he attends everything on his patch "just in case".

I had read a good deal in the papers about the coursing of live hares. It had, and still has, a lot of enemies, particularly among Socialist Members of Parliament. Attempts have been made since 1924 to place an Anti-Coursing Bill upon the statute book but, to date, all have failed. I knew that the political atmosphere surrounding the sport could lead to some aggravation, but was that likely to happen at Aidensfield?

Against that background, therefore, I attended my first coursing meeting. Sergeant Blaketon advised me to be on the alert for trouble because he had learned of a similar meeting, in Lancashire, where a crowd of anti-blood sport fanatics had demonstrated. They had invaded the coursing field into the bargain. Chaos had resulted, with some violence from all parties and I was warned against a repetition of that. Chaos must not occur at Aidensfield, ordered Sergeant Blaketon.

In uniform, with wellies on my feet, I walked down to the course. It was held on the flat fields of Home Farm. These were spacious grassy areas, although some were of stubble, and all were bounded by trees and interesting copses. They provided good running for both dogs and hares, and I was happy to learn that there were adequate parking facilities, with ample space for the roving crowds. Spectators at coursing meetings do not stand still, but wander around to see the action. The action depends greatly upon the location of the hares which are the focal-point of the sport.

Another feature of the place was the mobile canteen and its supplies of hot soup, meat pies and sausage rolls. Next door stood the mobile liquor bar, and although it was only ten o'clock in the morning, it was open and serving alcoholic refreshment designed to warm the cockles of anyone's heart. The necessary licence had been obtained – I checked that. The arena was growing busier by the minute.

The essence of this misunderstood sport is that of hunting a hare with a greyhound. The sport has persisted since the beginning of time and the first laws of coursing were drawn up in the sixteenth century. The modern sport, however, differs from the ancient in that the killing of a hare does not necessarily determine the winning dog. Many enemies of the sport believe that this is one of the rules – it is not, as I was to learn from that day's duty.

Mingling with the spectators and competitors, I watched the sequence of events and soon the objects of the sport and the marking system became reasonably clear. I was helped by the chap who served the beer on the make-shift bar and learned that he was secretary of the local club. It was affiliated to the Old Yorkshire Coursing Club which had closed forty-eight years before this meeting, but which had been revived only a year earlier. The headquarters of that club were also at a pub.

With the barman, whose name was Sid, I watched the prelude to the day's events. A long line of beaters, each equipped with a white flag and a good voice, were despatched into the distance. When they were some 400 or 500 yards away, each man smartly about-turned and began to advance towards the clear field before us. This was the coursing field, an area set aside for the purpose. The beaters spread themselves across the width of the countryside and began to wallop the undergrowth with the flags and short sticks, shouting and making a terrible din. Ahead of them was the coursing field where two competing greyhounds were held on slip-leads. The object was to locate a hare and drive it into the field so that it would be seen by the eager dogs. Only two dogs compete in each course. These fit, shivering animals were therefore waiting for the first hare to come bounding into the flat field, whereupon, at a signal from the judge, they would be slipped from their leads by the slipper. The judge was mounted on a horse to give clarity of vision and ease of movement as the dogs chased the hare around that field. From the moment the dogs are slipped, the course is on.

As was expected, there were several abortive beats and on one occasion that day, a leveret was put up. For those not familiar with rural life, a leveret is a young hare, but he was allowed his freedom. Coursing is for fit, adult hares only.

Eventually, a suitable hare was put up. A signal came from one of the beater's white flags which was held aloft for all to see, and the beaters began to warble as only coursing beaters can. The expectant crowd waited for the hare to bolt through the hedge and into the coursing field. He was driven that way by the oncoming beaters and their horrendous voices; finally, he entered through the hedge, ears flat against his body as he raced for his life. He legged it for all he was worth, heading for the far side of the arena and darting across the frontage of spectators. When he was about two hundred yards ahead of the straining dogs, they were slipped. The first course was on.

At this point, I learned of the two great differences between greyhound racing and coursing. Firstly, the hare in coursing is a live one; he is on his home ground, unconfined open countryside which he knows intimately and which he uses to good advantage. The second difference is that the dogs operate only in pairs, and they are identified by colours. One wears red and the other wears white.

Because the competition begins with the slipping, the judge has the unenviable task of deciding the winner and it is invariably a very close contest. The judge on this occasion was a lady, the only woman qualified as a coursing judge in the North of England. She had to award points for speed in get-away, for the number of times the dog makes the hare turn, for go-byes (overtaking of one dog by the other in the chase), and for the lengths distant from the hare. Points are also awarded for toppling the hare, but not for a kill. A kill does not determine the winning dog. In fact, a kill can lose the course because the other dog can gain valuable points during the killer's excitement. If a kill does occur, the course ends there, but it usually occurs when the hare escapes through the hedge and runs out of the coursing field. At this point, a trained coursing greyhound will return to its owner. Usually, coursing greyhounds are kept solely for this purpose and are not run in other races.

During all the meetings I attended in the course of my police duty, I never saw one hare killed or maimed. As a matter of interest, it is a strict rule that only wild hares are used for the sport. It is against coursing rules to breed hares or to use captive hares for this purpose. Another rule forbids the coursing of ground to which hares have been introduced within the last six months. This allows the animals time to acquaint themselves with their natural surroundings. Some clubs will not chase hares which are wet due to the rain. They like their hares to be in peak condition – it helps the hares and it provides a better test of skill for the dogs. Hares are always given between 150 and 200 yards start too.

I must admit that I was impressed by the rigid rules which govern the sport, and after talking to the followers I was pleased to learn that they do their utmost to obey those rules. They are very conscious of the propaganda being issued against the sport and ask only that the true facts be known to a wider audience.

The judge, at the end of each course, raises either a red flag or a white one to indicate the winning dog; if the result is a draw, the judge raises his (or her) riding cap. The judge wears hunting pink.

At this meeting, sixteen dogs were waiting to participate, and at £5 per entry, the prize money was good. The victorious dog is the only one who has beaten all others during the day's competition, having knocked out all competitors as the meeting progresses. The winning dog of each heat competes against the following dog, but on a bad day, not every dog will get his chance. It depends upon the number of hares found; hares are not always available and cannot be made to appear to order.

The ultimate in the coursing world in this country is the Waterloo Cup, held each February at Altcar, near Liverpool. This was instituted in 1836 by the proprietor of the Waterloo Hotel in Liverpool, and the winning of that cup is the dream

of every coursing fanatic. But even our little meeting attracted its share of enthusiasts – they came from all over
Great Britain, including Scotland and Ireland.

But, as O.B. had predicted, the meeting also attracted
unwelcome attention. As the day progressed, I became aware
of alien visitors, people carrying placards and waving banners
which condemned coursing and all who followed it. I realised
they were there about two-thirty in the afternoon and as it
would grow dark before five, I was not too alarmed. The
meeting would end about four o'clock, I felt, so I decided to
keep a wary eye on the visitors. I would inform the organisers
if trouble appeared likely. I noticed the protestors were long-
haired, youthful and serious; they did not dress like country-
folk, and they did not enter the coursing area. They remained
on the road outside the farm, having apparently learned
something of the laws of trespass on private property. Had
they trespassed on that field during the day, the farmer would
have been within his rights to eject them or at least ask them
to leave. He allowed coursing spectators and participants
upon his land, but did not permit enemies of the sport to
enter, consequently they could be considered trespassers.

Clearly, they realised this and as the afternoon progressed,
the little gathering of protestors grew to around twenty. They
had chosen their location fairly well because everyone who
left the coursing meeting, whether by vehicle or on foot,
would have to pass them and read their messages or listen to
their words of wisdom. The sporting Press were there too, but
whether they would photograph these people remained in
doubt. The local reporter was there, but he did not warrant
the assistance of a photographer. It seemed that their protest
would be limited to the spectators and a few villagers, and I
knew they would all ignore it.

Happily, the demonstration was a peaceful one. I wandered
over to the group to acquaint myself with them and found
them charming and sincere, an interesting group of earnest
youngsters, male and female, none of whom had ever attended a coursing meeting and none of whom had studied the
rules. Nonetheless, they believed they had a right to make
their protest and I could not forbid them, unless they ob-
structed the highway or broke the law in some other way. I

did not wish to chase them away, for everyone must have the right to free speech and thought, so long as it does not infringe upon the freedom of others.

I returned to the meeting for the final minutes and then Sergeant Blaketon arrived.

"What's that lot at the road end?" he asked, indicating with his head.

"Protestors," I told him. "They've come to demonstrate against coursing."

"Are they a nuisance?" he put to me.

"No, Sergeant," and I explained their activities and intentions.

"They can't hang around here all night," he commented.

"They won't," I assured him. "The meeting ends about four o'clock and I'm sure they'll leave then. They've got scooters with them."

"Don't stand any nonsense from them," he ordered me. "Remember you can book them for obstruction of the highway if they block the road. And there's breach of the peace if they fight."

"I'll remember, Sergeant," and off he went to have a look at the final contest of the day. I remained near the gate, keeping half an eye on the protestors and half on the progress of the meeting. As the final race got under way, I saw the protestors group themselves into a formidable knot and squat right in the centre of the exit road! I groaned. This was exactly what I did not want. This could cause trouble.

This kind of thing had been done before. Demonstrators would squat in the middle of the road, a most effective ploy, and they brought traffic to a halt. With Press and photographers there, the situation could be guaranteed publicity and this was beneficial to their cause. Invariably, those protested against would react violently and that would damage their image. With only two policemen at this meeting, as fast as we removed one protestor, another would take his place. Two policemen could not forcibly remove twenty sit-down demonstrators. The spectators' cars would be forced to stop and frustration would build up into something serious. If the protestors were manhandled by anyone except the police, they would register complaints of assault. And this was the only exit route from the field. I couldn't direct the leaving crowds via another route. I was sure that if I left the sit-downers in position, the trapped and frustrated spectators would use their own methods of dispersal. And that would mean trouble – big trouble, with lots of unwelcome publicity.

I looked at my watch. It was ten minutes to four.

Already cars were forming a queue at the exit of the car park and within minutes, they would arrive at this blockage. I decided to address the group.

"O.K. lads," I began. "You've made your point. Now move on, please, and let these people go home."

"We're not moving until we get an assurance that there will be no further coursing meetings here,"m said their spokesman, a clean-faced youngster with freckles and bright blue eyes.

"I'm afraid you will have to move," I chose my words carefully.

"It will take more than you and your sergeant to shift us," said another, a thick-set youth with a bushy beard. He looked like a prop forward.

"You said it," I smiled, and returned to the field. Sergeant Blaketon came towards me, looking very harassed.

"They're there, Rhea, look at them! They'll sit there and block the road until they've got publicity. If we're not careful, there'll be a punch-up. Some of these chaps have had a skin full of ale . . ."

"We needn't worry, Sergeant," I said confidently. "They'll soon go," and I told him the reason why I was so sure. He smiled and nodded his approval to my idea. I then moved towards the first car in the queue and explained the situation to him, asking him to be patient for about ten minutes. He agreed. I told the driver of the car behind and got the motorists to pass back the word. They smiled and were happy at my suggestions.

And so the protestors sat in the middle of the exit road, with a queue of very patient, smiling motorists confronting them, with engines idle and with no blaring horns. I waited too, and I must admit I was a little apprehensive. The seconds ticked away. Four o'clock came and went. And then at three minutes past four, I knew I had won.

Farmer Joe Sculley was bringing his cows in. They moved

slowly and inexorably towards the little band of demonstrators, their horned heads down and their tails lashing as they deposited pounds of wet cow-clap behind them along their route. Those cows had no intention of stopping for this little party and ploughed on, thinking only of the blessed relief of the milking parlour.

In the face of this opposition, the demonstrators left their positions and the leading car moved deftly into position right behind the cows, spreading the fertiliser evenly across the highway. The queue of cars moved slowly away behind the trudging cows, and so we won the day.

It would take a very dedicated demonstrator to squat in a sea of freshly deposited cow dung.

Four

I became fascinated at the number of craftsmen who managed to earn a living on my beat. Almost every village or hamlet boasted one or more of these interesting folk. There was the cobbler of Elsinby, the woodcarver of Aidensfield, the blacksmith of Maddleskirk, the potter of Crampton, the furniture-maker of Briggsby and a host of assorted artists, writers and sculptors.

I found these people just as interesting as the farmers and rurals with whom I worked, and I respected them because of their independence, their love of hard work and their undying spirit. In their own way, they had discarded what is often termed the "rat race", and had settled in this rural paradise to earn their living in the way they wished. Pensions and status meant nothing to them, and they seemed to avoid the pressures of modern life. I was envious of them and their freedom.

I did not discover all these people at once. It took me some months to appreciate the wealth of talent that lay within the boundaries of my beat and I made new discoveries of this sort almost weekly. The first realisation that I had someone of note living nearby came with the arrival of a huge lorry. It parked outside my house one afternoon while I was off duty, enjoying a spot of weeding. The driver hailed me and announced he was seeking a Mr James Flagg who had a quarry.

"There's no one of that name with a quarry around here," I told him, racking my brains to recall such a person.

"Well," said the driver. "I've got a delivery note that says there is. 'James Flagg, Aidensfield', it says. And I've got a bloody great lump of rock for him."

He pointed to the rock in question. It was massive. I did wonder why he'd be taking rock *to* a quarry, but didn't ask – there must have been a logical reason.

"There's only one quarry around here," I pointed out. "It's down the road at Thackerston. It's a limestone quarry, getting rid of lumps like that after it's been broken down to powder."

"I've been there," he said. "It's not theirs."

Being new to the village, I decided to ask Mary if she'd heard of Flagg. She'd met many villagers socially. "Darling," I called through the door. "Have we anybody called Flagg in the village?"

"Yes," she replied. "I've met her, she's got a youngster at play-school. She plays with our Elizabeth. Nice people. They live in that little cottage at the far end of the village. Honeysuckle Cottage."

I knew the house. It was a gorgeous cottage built into the lee of a hill; it faced south with roses and honeysuckle around the doorway and was everyone's ideal country home.

"There's a Mr Flagg down the village," I pointed out the route. "But it's not a quarry. He's a sculptor – he carves things out of stone and wood."

I had seen him at work as I passed his house, but hadn't connected the name with him until now.

"How am I going to get this lump off my truck then? I thought I was taking it to a quarry – I thought there'd be lifting gear . . . "

I walked to the gate for a closer look at his load. Strapped onto the flat rear of his lorry was a huge oblong piece of stone. It was a good eight feet long by six feet high and six feet wide. It was secured with heavy ropes and stood on a pad of thick rubber material. It had come from somewhere in the Scottish Highlands and was beautiful to behold. I don't know what type of stone it was, but even in its square untouched state, it looked magnificent. Having made sure the driver knew the location of Honeysuckle Cottage, I waved him into a lane to turn his long vehicle.

"I hope that chap's got lifting gear," he shouted as he moved off.

"If he's expecting you, he'll have something fixed up, I'm sure," I called after him, hopefully.

I must confess that my curiosity had been aroused and fortuitously I had some mail to post. This seemed an ideal time to potter down the village and drop them in the letter box. I dressed in some passable clothes which were not full of soil and stray rose thorns, and meandered upon my little expedition.

From the distance, I could see the lorry parked outside Honeysuckle Cottage and could see the figure of the driver gesticulating; before him stood the squat shape of the sculptor, listening carefully. They walked around the lofty chunk of rock, each looking seriously at the vehicle and doubtless discussing mutual problems. I pushed my letters into the box and went into the post office to buy some stamps, a pair of bootlaces, some sugar and a bag of firelighters. When I emerged, they were still there, walking around the lorry like a pair of dogs sniffing a butcher's van.

I wished I dare walk closer, but refrained because it would seem I was snooping. But a shout from one of them halted me.

"Mr Rhea!" It was not the lorry driver's voice. I stopped, turned around and walked the fifty yards or so towards the unhappy pair.

"Mr Rhea? Our new policeman?" the man asked me.

"I am."

"James Flagg. I'm a sculptor, as you may know. I've a problem," and he looked at the vehicle and its load.

"Is it yours?"

"Mine," he smiled wryly. "All the way from Scotland and would you believe, they've sent it on a flat lorry. No crane. They always send a lorry with lifting gear. What can I do? It must not be cracked or chipped in any way. It's for a commissioned piece – a Madonna and Child . . . "

"How much does it weigh?" I asked.

"Several tons," said the driver. "I'm not sure really, except it's a bloody great lump of stone."

"You've not had this problem before?" I asked Flagg, hoping he might provide his own solution.

"Never. Mind you, this is the biggest chunk I've ordered for a long time, and they've always sent a lorry with lifting gear. Always. They know my requirements."

"There's Paddy Stone at Maddleskirk," I suggested.

"Stone? That's appropriate!" laughed Flagg. "Who's he?"

"He's got the timber yard there. I had him remove a fallen oak a few weeks ago. He came out with a massive crane and shifted it in no time. I'll bet that oak weighed as much as your lump of stone."

"Is he on the telephone?"

"He must be," I said.

Flagg rushed inside and made his call. It seemed that Paddy was at work in his timber yard and being the generous man that he was, he accepted the challenge. It was a ten-minute drive out to Aidensfield, and he came with two of his best men, plus an impressive crane.

The problem was finding something to grip the rock without damaging it and then to lift it sufficiently to slide a powerful sling beneath. But Paddy did the trick. He used a type of jack which lifted the stone very gently and then slid a second one beneath it. By pumping a handle, he lifted the rock high enough to slide a strong belt beneath it, and he repeated this with other strong belts until he had the chunk in a type of cradle.

It was then a simple matter for the crane to hoist it from the lorry and deposit it in Flagg's front garden, at a point selected by him. We all went inside for a noggin of whisky and Paddy got himself a few quid for the job.

When I showed interest in Flagg's work, he showed me around his studio. He explained how a figure was created and how moulds were made for copies to be taken. His work appeared in many churches, both in Britain and Europe, and from that day I was welcome to call at any time. It was an offer that I frequently accepted. I would stand for minutes at a time, watching him chip away at featureless lumps of rock or timber, to create beautiful figures in his own distinctive style.

Over the months, I saw that huge lump of rock change shape. It lost its squareness and began to assume a more rounded outline, and then the features of a head began to appear. This was gradually followed by the familiar outline of a Madonna and Child, and by the end of the year, the figure was complete. It was beautiful, two human bodies with skin as smooth as any advert for expensive soap whose clothing bore all the creases and wrinkles that one expects in real life. The expression on the mother's face, the innocence in the baby's gaze – it was all contained in that solid lump of Scottish rock.

The next problem was moving it out. It had to travel down to London to the buyer who had commissioned it, and I was pleased to learn that Paddy was hired for the lifting ceremony. With infinite care and tenderness, he used his experience to manhandle that heavy, boxed load onto a lorry for transportation to the big city, two hundred and fifty miles away. Before it left, Flagg opened the crate to inspect his work, to ensure it was undamaged before leaving Aidensfield. I looked inside too, and so did the lorry driver, a stranger to the area.

He looked at the child's face, and then at Paddy.

"That's you, innit?" he smiled and the case was bolted shut.

Paddy blushed; I hadn't noticed the likeness, and James Flagg merely smiled. The load arrived safely at its destination and Paddy got more jobs after that. But I could hardly regard him as a face of innocence.

* * * *

Samuel Cook looked like a cobbler, which he was. I found him by accident. When walking through Elsinby one afternoon, the heel of my boot fell off and my embarrassment was witnessed by an elderly gentleman on his way to collect his pension.

"Nip into Aud Sam's," he advised. "He'll fix it for you."

He issued guidance to Sam's workshop so I hobbled the few hundred yards to locate it. It was half way up a steep hill which led from Elsinby towards Waindale. It was a wooden hut painted a deep green and somewhat isolated. Sam seemed happy out here, a good five minutes' walk from his home.

I limped to the door, knocked and waited. There was no reply, but I knew he was inside because I could hear the whirl of his sewing-machine. I knocked again. The noise stopped and the door opened. A small man about sixty years old with thick ginger hair greeted me. He had heavy spectacles with thick lenses and they were covered in dust. How he could see through that heavy layer, I do not know. He wore a thick, long apron of strong leather and several tin tacks were clamped between his lips, like vampire's fangs.

He muttered through them.

"Come in, nobody ever knocks, Just come in," so I followed him into the tiny workshop. To the left of his door was his store of new shoes and wellington boots, all for sale. They were stored neatly on racks, brown on one side of the hut and black on the other. There were no other colours. The big shelves held huge boots, tough shoes and leather leggings, all the trappings of country folk, while the smaller shelves bore the cobbler's accoutrements, like polish, laces, heels, dubbin, brushes and a host of other items. The entire place reeked of leather – the woodwork must be saturated with the scent, but it was not unpleasant.

In the centre of the floor stood an ancient but efficient wood-burning stove. This was Sam's heating system and waste disposal unit; when winter descended, I found it most reliable and welcoming. He used it to burn his waste products and rubbish, and I later discovered that he mended Paddy Stone's shoes, and did other leather work for him, all free of charge. This was in return for free loads of end-cuts from Paddy's timber yard. Sam would drive up in his van, deliver a pile of boots and shoes which Paddy repaired for his family and workmen, and in return Paddy would load Sam's van with pieces cut off the end of his timber. It seemed a marvellous working arrangement, although I often wondered what the tax man made of it.

To the right as you entered the hut was Sam's working area, containing the bench at which he spent all his working days. Here he had spent all his working life, cobbling for all he was worth and it seemed he demanded no more from society than the grace to allow him to continue his craft. He had a very old but beautifully made sewing-machine which looked as if it would never break down, and which thrived on a diet of thick thread and thin oil. The bench was piled high with leather pieces of all shapes and sizes, and knives hung from the wall. These were razor sharp with blades hollowed by sharpening over countless years. Many is the time I've watched him shape a heel from a piece of thick leather, marvelling at his swift and uncanny skill. That first day, I watched him hammer one home on a boot, skim the edges with a polishing wheel and then dye the new leather to match the existing boot. It looked so simple, but this was his craft. He worked day in and day out, never complaining.

I showed him the heel of my boot and he examined it. "You could do with a new 'un," he said simply, his brown face expressionless.

"I'll leave it," I said stupidly, for I had no spare.

"Nay, I'll fix it now," and he did. I sat on a chair near the stove with one stockinged foot on a stool as he shaped a heel for me. He tacked it onto my boot and trimmed the edges.

"How much?" I asked when he'd finished.

"Sixpence," was his price.

"Sixpence?" I gasped. It would have cost me a few shillings in town. "Here, take two bob."

But he refused. "I know my terms," he said proudly. "I'm not one for making a big profit. Big money brings its problems, you know. I just want to earn a decent living – a fair day's work for a fair day's pay."

He steadfastly refused even to take a sixpence as a tip. Today, a sixpence is worth $2\frac{1}{2}$ pence in decimalised currency. Naturally, I returned there often, with my police boots, the children's shoes, leather bags and a host of other items which required his skill. His charges for sewing up a split handbag or suitcase would be 2d or 3d; the full repair of a pair of shoes would be fifteen shillings or so, all of which were about a third of the price in York or elsewhere. And he was good too – plus the fact, he provided personal service.

Through calling regularly, I discovered he was seldom alone in his little shop. Everyone popped in for a sit beside his stove and a chat, but he worked through their chatter. He talked freely about his life, about shoeing the monks at nearby Maddleskirk Abbey, about making hunting boots, clogs, leather aprons and saddleware. He could fashion

almost anything from leather it seemed, but he had
another talent. I learned he was a hairdresser.

Practically all rural cobblers were hairdressers and his
charge was 3d (1½p) for a short-back-and-sides. I did not use
him for this purpose, except on one occasion. I had been
summoned to Police Headquarters for an interview with the
Chief Constable. It seemed that the Chief Constable had
telephoned my superintendent who telephoned the inspector
who telephoned Sergeant Blaketon.

O.B. rang me and instructed, "Rhea. Get yourself over to
Headquarters for two o'clock this afternoon. The Chief wants
to talk to you."

At that stage, no one told me what the Chief wanted to talk
about. O.B.'s instructions had been curt, and all manner of
possible reasons flashed before me. I was being posted away
from the beat. I had been promoted. I had made a mess of
something. There'd been a complaint about me. My hair was
too long . . .

Hair!

It was too long for an officer about to be interviewed by the
Chief Constable, so I had to get it cut in a hurry. I thought of
Sam and his cobbler's shop. He was salvation. I hadn't time
to go elsewhere. I drove across to Elsinby, went in and
explained the problem. He said he would cut my hair immediately and I settled on a chair. After covering me with the
traditional checked cloth, he snipped away at me, chattering
all the time and regaling me with tales about World War I. I
paid my 3d and went home for an early lunch. As I walked in,
Mary burst into fits of laughter.

"What on earth have you done!" she cried, with tears
streaming down her face. "It's like one of those pudding basin
cuts!"

And so it was. Sam didn't have the luxury of a mirror so I
hadn't been able to view myself before leaving his emporium.
In the comfort of my own home, the full horror of my hair
style was plain to see. My hair was like that of a village yokel
of the fifteenth century – and I was due to meet the Chief
within the hour. I tried trimming it with scissors, but it was
futile. I had to leave because it was a twenty-mile run on the
Francis Barnett. *En route,* I determined that I would not show

my back view to the Chief. If I was in trouble of any sort, this display would only aggravate matters.

With some trepidation, therefore, I waited hatless outside the Chief Constable's office door at Headquarters and was ushered in. I stood to attention, smart in my pressed uniform and clean shirt. I had done what I could with my hair at the front and I thought it had passed his scrutiny. He left his desk and came forward to shake hands with me. This surprised me.

"Congratulations, Rhea," he beamed. "You've done us proud. A splendid show. Excellent."

I must have looked surprised. Indeed I was, for I had no idea what I'd done to justify this reception. It was certainly not the hair-do.

"You don't know why you are here?" he must have recognised the look of bewilderment on my face.

"No, sir," I shook my head and felt the hair flop over my brow. I swallowed hard.

"The Gold Medal Essay. The Queen's Police Gold Medal Essay competition," he said proudly. "You submitted an essay on juvenile delinquency."

"Yes, sir," my heart began to thump.

"You've got second prize, Rhea. You were beaten by the Commissioner of the South Australia Police. It was a Commonwealth competition, Rhea, with entries from all over the world. And you've got second prize. Here is a cheque for £30 – I am delighted. I regard this as a triumph for the force."

The Home Office, who arranged the competition, had apparently notified my Force direct, and I had no idea of this success. I accepted the cheque gratefully, for it represented almost three weeks pay. With three little children, we needed every penny, so I was delighted. After a chat about the work I'd put into the essay, he dismissed me. I wheeled smartly about, stomped my feet and marched from his office.

Then a loud bellow halted me. "Rhea!"

"Sir?" I was only inches from the door.

"What the bloody hell's happened to your hair?"

I turned to face him. "I had it cut this morning, sir, in a rush."

"What a bloody awful mess! I'm amazed at you, reporting here like that. I'm amazed that you had the effrontery to enter my office in a state of that kind. God Almighty! I wouldn't be seen dead like that, man," and he proceeded to give me the bulling of my life. He was expert at this, being an ex-military man, and I left his office clutching my cheque for £30, but feeling as small and as helpless as a harvest mouse. His dressing-down made me shake for hours afterwards.

I often returned to Sam's workshop, where I talked to him and had my shoes repaired, but I never let him touch another hair of my head.

* * * *

I met another of my craftsmen friends during routine enquiries into a series of housebreakings in the locality. Someone had been travelling around the villages in the early afternoon of certain weekdays, and had broken into several houses over a wide area of the district. Individually, the thefts were not very serious – at each house, two or three pounds in cash would be removed from tins on mantel-shelves, or food would be taken from the larders. Occasionally, an item of clothing would disappear and very infrequently, something with a saleable value would be missed, like a portable radio or small items of jewellery. Taken as a whole, however, the crimes were serious and engendered considerable alarm among the people.

My detective colleagues had investigated these crimes, many of which had occurred well beyond the boundaries of my beat and concluded they were the work of either a tramp or someone on the run, living locally and stealing in order to survive. It could be the work of absconders from an approved school, but the pattern ruled out a professional thief bent on stealing high-value goods.

As time went by without an arrest, the women folk began to grow alarmed at the prospect of someone entering their homes and rifling through their belongings. I made a point, therefore, of visiting as many isolated houses as possible, in an attempt to alert the occupants to the criminal's activities. It was during one of those missions that I came across Stanley George Hatton.

I discovered his house after bouncing my motor-cycle along

an unkept lane for almost a mile. It was a very isolated place, and a sign on the gate said 'Brockrigg Farm'. I entered and drove the motor-cycle as far as possible along the muddy track, then parked it against a stone gate post. I removed my helmet and walked the final twenty-five yards to the house. I knocked on the door and waited. Soon I heard heavy footsteps inside and a woman's voice told a dog to "Git oot o' t'rooad" before the door opened.

"Oh!" upon seeing me, she smoothed her rough hessian apron, known hereabouts as a 'cooarse appron', and said, "Oh, it's t'bobby."

"Yes," I said. "I've come to give advice about burglars."

"Here?" The dog appeared and sniffed at me. It was one of the black-and-white curs which are so prominent in the farms of the region.

"Hereabouts," I told her. I called the criminal a *burglar* whereas the term was strictly wrong. He was a *housebreaker* because he broke in during the daylight hours. Burglars were those who broke and entered houses during the night, but since that time, the law has changed. All those who break into premises of any kind are now legally entitled to the name of burglar. It is a technicality, but the word *burglar* has always been easily understood by the general public.

"Well you'd better have a chat wiv oor Stanley George," she suggested.

"Your husband?"

"Aye, he's roond there, in yon aud barn, working."

"Thanks," and I followed the direction of her finger.

The large double-sided barn door was open and I walked in. I expected to find a farmer hard at work, but instead I found a carpenter. The old barn had been converted into a comfortable work-shop and it was full of wooden articles. My first impression was that of a furniture store, but the scent of glue and polish, of wood shavings and of oak told me otherwise. There was a mass of wood shavings on the floor too, and rows of tools hung from the wall. This was a one-man factory.

A stiff man in late middle age got up from the bench and struggled towards me, limping painfully.

"Don't, I'll come over," and I crossed the floor towards him.

He smiled gratefully, and settled back on the stool beside the bench.

"Rheumatics," he said wryly. "In me aud legs. Gives me hell, it does."

"I'm P.C. Rhea," I said, holding out a hand. He shook it strongly.

"Hatton," he introduced himself. "Stanley George Hatton. Everybody calls me Stanley George. It's on account of my mother. She had three lads, me and two brothers. She called 'em all Stanley because it was her favourite name – I'm Stanley George, there's Stanley Eric and Stanley Peter. I wish folks would just call me George, but they never do, not around here."

I settled on a newly made chair at his side and explained the reason for my visit. He listened intently and said he'd make sure everything was locked up. In any case, he and his wife were always pottering about the premises during the day, and she'd notice any strangers lurking about. We talked happily and his wife, whose name I learned was Millie, brought us a cup of tea. She stopped for a chat, and I told her of my mission. She had heard about the thefts and house-breakings and promised to be a little more crime-conscious.

I had a look around his workshop and marvelled at the quality of his work. There were chairs galore, Windsor style in the main, which he had fashioned from the piles of wood stacked in one corner. But he had also made cupboards, wardrobes, even bedsteads and a whole range of large items like dining-suites and kitchen-fittings. He told how he had been compelled to give up farming because of his legs. He'd let his land to neighbours but not being a man for idling his time away, he'd turned to his life-long hobby of carpentry. Suddenly, the orders had boomed – he found himself making complete dining-sets for customers, and Windsor chairs which sold rapidly to the city stores, and a host of other items. He'd had offers of more than enough work and had been surprised to suddenly find himself in demand. He worked to suit himself and accepted jobs which meant he could remain seated for much of the time. All his work was hand-finished and polished with a care that bordered on the fanatical.

I began calling on him every time I was in Briggsby, once a

quarter or so, and we had long, interesting talks. Gradually, I realised his farm was not connected to the mains electricity supply; he had no electrical apparatus in his workshop and even his drill was hand operated. His wife cooked on a large Aga in her ample kitchen and the light came from oil lamps strategically placed about the premises. The whole farm had an air of calmness and peace, very reminiscent of the last century.

I grew very fond of Stanley George and Millie. He would chat away to me in the rich dialect of the locality, and I could chatter back in like terms. I told him about life in a modern police force, with motor vehicles, personal radio sets and improved facilities. He told me about the old days on the farm, before tractors came along and before combine harvesters had shortened the harvest period.

It was some months later that Stanley George sought my advice on a matter which was troubling him.

"Thoo's a man of the world," he said one day as we drank Millie's tea. "I'd like a spot of advice."

"Of course," I assured him. "Ask any time."

"Well, it's like this," he began, sipping slowly from his mug. "We've no 'lectric in this house. We've grown used to makking do wivoot it, me and oor Millie. Never missed it, you understand. Onnyrooad, some 'lectric fellers were fixing poles and cables just over that hill behind our house. Last week, this was. Yan on 'em come to me and asked if I wanted t'electric in this house. He's given me till this weekend to think it over."

"And do you want it?" I put to him.

"Nay, now I can't be sure," he admitted. "Just can't mak up my mind. I mean, what good would it be to me, at this stage of life?"

"It would make life easier," I assured him. "You'd have instant light all around the house, you could boil kettles of water much faster, you could have power tools in here, like drills and saws."

"It would tak me ages ti get accustomed ti it."

"What about Millie? How's she feel about it?"

"No idea," he shook his head. "She's no idea. She's got relations in Richmond with t'electric, but they burn t'toast, t'custard gits tak tiv it, and all soorts goes wrong. And them bulbs they use – they keep banging and flashing."

"Faulty wiring, I'll bet," I said. "If lights keep flashing or bulbs keep blowing, it'll be old wiring. They should get new wiring fitted right through the house. But back to you – I reckon you'd like it."

"Them 'lectric fellers said they'd fix me up wiv an estimate," he said. "What's that mean?"

"It means they'll come around your house and buildings to examine everything, and then tell you what's needed – how much wire, for example, how many plugs and sockets they recommend and that sort of thing. The Electricity Board will send you a letter telling you what it will cost."

"And would I have to get it?"

"Not if you didn't want to," I assured him. "The estimate will be free – they come along and measure up, that's all. For nowt."

"They said they would come this Friday, unless I said no."

"Let them come," I said. "At least you'll know what it will cost you. You might say no when you learn what the cost is, but at least you'll have an opportunity to be fitted with electricity."

Stanley George agreed to this. I left him and it was another fortnight before I returned to his farm. I popped into his workshop as usual, and the inevitable cup of tea appeared. Millie stayed with us for a chat.

"Well?" I asked him. "Did they estimate for your electricity?"

"By!" he said with feeling. "By, that was a to-do, that was. Two fellers came with rulers and instruments and they went right round that house of mine, and right round these buildings. It took 'em ages, I can tell you. They went through ivvery room doonstairs, and then upstairs. I was right behind, watching from t'bottom to t'top, and do you know, they started to measure every bedroom. Well, Mr Rhea, we've seven bedrooms in this aud house, and I can't see t'sense in having 'lectric in every room, can you?"

"It's the normal practice," I told him.

"It seems daft to me," he shook his head. "I reckon all I would need would be one light on t'landing. It would shine into ivvery room upstairs, eh? I can't see t'sense in having lights in every bedroom."

"It's convenience," I said. "You enter your bedroom, switch on the light and get ready for bed . . ."

"Aye," he said, "That's it. I like reading in bed, and so does our Millie. Just imagine – we'd get settled in, all nice and snug, and then we'd have to get out and paddle across t'floor to put t'lights out. By my way of thinking, if we had one light on that landing, it would show us upstairs and we could use candles at our bedsides, like we allus have. We could switch t'landing light off, take our candles across to t'bedside and read till we felt like nodding off. Then blow t'candles out. That way, you keep your feet warm."

Try as I might, I could not convince him that it was better to have lights in every room, nor could he appreciate the value of an overhead switch at the bedhead. I do not know what his estimated cost was, but he did tell me it was based on a full system downstairs, with power and light installed in his workshop, but only one light on the stairs. There were to be no lights in the bedrooms. He'd made his mind up about that, and the estimate was made on those terms.

He had the electricity installed to his desire. I called late one afternoon and learned it had been in working order for about ten days. The men had wired the house and he had a solitary bulb, without a shade, at the top of the staircase, from where it shone into all seven bedrooms. He had relented a little because the bathroom contained an electric bulb. Downstairs, the system was complete and Millie had a brand new washing machine, cooker, kettle, iron and other essential modern household goods. It must have cost Stanley George a fortune, but I knew he was well off.

"Well?" I asked, settling at his side. "How's the new electricity?"

"I don't reckon much to it," he said bluntly. "Our Millie still cooks on that Aga, it's hot all t'time you see. And that cup of tea – well, that aud kettle boils on that Aga, all t'time, so it's allus ready. Bubbling away all day, singing and warm. And she puts her iron on before she fettles my shirts and things . . . we don't use t'electric, you know. We don't need it."

"Not at all?" I cried. "Not after all that expense?"

"I can't use it in my workshop, Mr Rhea – I like a hand drill and hand tools. They've got feeling in 'em, you see. Power tools have no feeling, have they?"

"But surely you must make some use of it?"

"Aye," he acknowledged gravely. "We do. That light on t'top of our stairs. We switch it on before going up to bed. It lights our way upstairs and we switch it off before we go into our bedrooms. That's a very useful light, is that one."

I called upon him many times after that, but I never saw him, or Millie, make use of anything electrical.

Incidentally, the youth responsible for the housebreakings was caught a month or so after my first contact with Stanley George. He'd run away from home and was sleeping in a barn about eight miles away, living by his thefts.

*　　　*　　　*　　　*

Perhaps my favourite craftsman was Aud John. Everyone knew him as Aud John and it was some time before I knew his surname was Frankland. John was the local blacksmith at Maddleskirk and he had occupied his smithy just off the High Street for over seventy years. It had been his father's place before that, and John continued to operate with huge bellows, a pile of coke and an anvil which must have shaped thousands of horseshoes over many dozens of years.

John was well over eighty. He was a thick-set man and weighed well over seventeen stone. He had a fresh complexion, a white moustache and white hair with sparkling grey eyes. He habitually wore a long leather apron which was scorched with heat and tattered from other labours. He worked day in, day out with his sleeves rolled up and I never once saw him wear a jacket. His feet always sported clogs; he was muscular and fit, as straight as the proverbial ramrod and he possessed a marvellous sense of humour. Everyone liked and respected Aud John.

In his heyday, the smithy had been the resort of horses from far and near, and that had been the sole living of John and his father. John had continued to earn a good living until that period after World War II when horses began to dwindle as a form of rural draught and transport. The motor-vehicle was taking over and John found business sliding from him. He was not one for letting things go and refused to give up his ancient craft. After all, it was his only skill. He began to fashion ornamental gates and other similar fittings, which he sold at the markets of Harrowby, Brantsford and Ashfordly. Business began to thrive once again, although he still shod the occasional horse when the occasion demanded. With a renewed interest in horses, John's business enjoyed a second revival and he became busier than ever in his declining years. He reckoned that hard work kept him alive and fit. I believe it did.

I enjoyed visiting John. It was a long time before he totally accepted me, and I learned very quickly that he hated being watched at work. If he had a caller, he would promptly cease work and talk for as long as he considered necessary. He would then dismiss the visitor. As he worked in the open air in a square yard which abutted a lane running off the High Street, he had frequent interruptions, although I did discover that his trusted friends and local colleagues were allowed to talk to him while he worked.

My visits to his yard were originally for duty purposes. I was checking for stolen scrap metal. Unscrupulous scrap merchants might attempt to sell stolen property to him, or they might attempt to steal his stock of metal, consequently I paid regular visits to his small establishment, just to keep an eye on him and his belongings. Constant reminders kept him alert to the possibility of visits by criminals.

The entrance to his tiny square yard was through two wooden gates, just wide enough to admit a lorry, and these were always closed when he was working. He would sit or stand in a small clearing among his heaps of metal and there fashion his exquisite gates, brackets, fireplaces and other objects, many of which had been commissioned. Gradually, he began to accept me; I knew I had 'arrived' when he continued to work in my presence.

At the back of the yard was his store-room and internal workshop; inside the workshop was the traditional blacksmith's shop, with the anvil, the coke fire, the trough of water and piles of horseshoes. There was the ever-present smell of hot metal, coke and horses. On cold days, I would pop into that shop to get warm because the fire was always burning.

There is nothing cosier than a working blacksmith's shop.

One late autumn day, I popped in for a warm-up, for I'd been on a long motor-cycle patrol and was chilled to the core. Aud John nodded me through and I went across his yard and through to the shop where I removed my motor-cycle gear. I settled before the glowing fire, pumped the bellows to bring up a blaze, and warmed myself before it. Outside, John was busy with a wrought-iron gate which had to be finished that day, so I did not try to talk to him. I sat in his smithy while he worked outside, even though there was a hint of frost in the air.

And as I enjoyed the growing warmth, I became aware of two young men. They were strangers to the village and were leaning upon his gates, watching him at work. For a long time, he was unaware of their presence and I wondered how he would react when he realised they were there. I began to observe them, realising I was invisible to them within the darkness of the forge. The confrontation could be interesting.

Each visitor was about thirty years old, smartly dressed and obviously of good standing. One had thick fair hair and rimless glasses, while the other was rather thick-set with a balding head. Finally, John realised they were there.

"What's thoo fellers want?" he demanded, downing his tools with evident determination.

"Oh, er, nothing," the fair-haired one answered. "We are just watching."

"I'm a busy chap, and I don't like being watched by strangers," he told them. "Can I sell you anything?"

"No, thanks," the fair one said. "Can we watch for a while?"

Grudgingly, John retrieved his tools and resumed work on the urgent gate. He was uneasy, I could sense that. He continually looked across at them and I knew he wouldn't normally have worked like this, but the job was pressing. They remained leaning across his gate for a few more minutes, quietly observing his efforts. Finally, he could stand it no longer.

"Look here," he pulled himself to his full height, a magnificent man for his age. "I can't abide folks watching me when I'm working. If there's summat you want, then get it and leave me be. I've got to finish this job."

The balding one spoke.

"We're sorry," he smiled gently. "We'll go in a moment. But we find it so nice to watch a genuine craftsman at work, especially a man like you, working in the open air. We are up here on business, you see; we're heading for Brantsford and we stopped here to stretch our legs. We have a factory in the south; we're from London and we manufacture precision instruments. For that reason, it's so nice to find a real craftsman, working in the old tradition and using his own hands."

"That's right," his fair-haired companion continued. "Mind you, our sort of work is very, very precise. We have to work to an accuracy of one ten-thousandth of an inch."

"In that case," said John with his eyes twinkling, "You'd better stay and watch. I'm exact."

Five

With about a dozen Acts of Parliament and other minor pieces of legislation to cater for dogs, I realised the rich man's guardian and poor man's friend would feature in my daily work at Aidensfield. My beat was the home of numerous dogs and in common with other rural areas, they ranged from tiny indoor pets like Yorkshire terriers to keen, working and sporting dogs, but included the inevitable strays, sheep worriers, lost dogs and perpetual wanderers, to say nothing of Claude Jeremiah Greengrass's lurcher.

So far as the law was concerned, there were dog licences to check, stray dogs to house, sheep killers to be concerned about and collars to examine. Almost every week involved me in some form of doggy problem.

Due to this regular commitment, it wasn't long before I knew many of the resident dogs by their first names. I began to accept the situation that it was not unusual in this type of rural bliss, for dogs to wander unaccompanied around the villages. Each did its own thing while its unseen master went about his unknown business.

One such wanderer was Rufus, a lethargic Golden Labrador, whose unquenchable lust was for dustbins. He roamed Aidensfield at all hours, up-turning the district's dustbins so he could ferret among the contents. His master was a hairy musician who knew of Rufus's craving and who had tried, many many times, to cure him of the habit. Practically everyone else in the village had tried and while most of them had resorted to concealment of their bins, one man had gone to the lengths of wiring his bin to a 12-volt car battery. His hope was that Rufus would cock his leg against it or otherwise attempt to overturn it, and thus give himself a severe shock in a painful region. But Rufus never went near

79

that bin. He must have realised it was dangerous and it was an unfortunate refuse collector who received a nasty kick from the lethal object.

As Rufus went along his merry way, leaving as his trademark many up-skittled bins and trails of rubbish, Sergeant Blaketon instructed me to check all dog licences. Everytime I saw a dog, I must interview its owner to check the necessary document. It was around this time that the law changed slightly in favour of those farmers who kept dogs purely for working purposes. Hitherto, they had been permitted to keep a number of unlicensed dogs, based on the number of livestock they kept. Each year, these farmers required a certificate of exemption and came to the police for issue of the document. The change meant that any dog used solely for tending sheep or cattle could be kept without a licence and no certificate was necessary. The onus rested upon the farmer to prove that his dogs were for tending sheep or cattle, and even pups might be included under that general heading if they were being 'brought on' by older dogs. Among the people who could (and still can) keep dogs without licences were blind persons who kept guide dogs, persons keeping dogs under six months old, shepherds who kept dogs in the exercise of their calling, and keepers of hound dogs under 12 months of age, not having run with a pack.

I knew it would take weeks to check every dog licence on my beat, so I went into the four village post offices and, casually in the course of our small talk, I told the men and women behind the counters that it was my intention next week to check all dog licences. I knew the outcome – word would spread like wildfire that the bobby was having a purge and there would be a sudden rush of applications. I knew my ruse had worked because in the days which followed, several farmers came for advice about the new rules, and I later discovered the post offices had done a roaring trade in new issues. To satisfy Sergeant Blaketon's desire for correct procedures. I did check a few and recorded them in my notebook. It kept the sergeant happy and also showed the village that I had meant business. This piece of strategy was necessary because there might, in the future, be a reason for letting a similar piece of confidential information loose upon the villagers. A follow-up, however minor, was important in any ruse of this kind.

To accommodate the numbers of stray dogs that roam the nation, many police stations possess what is conveniently known as a dog house. Some rely on local dogs' homes, but official police dog houses come in varying shapes and sizes. Unfortunately, architectural ignorance invariably sites them next door to the cells or beneath the windows of private houses which adjoin police stations. Because the captured strays howl their protests long and loud at all hours of the day and night, this leads to complaints from prisoners who say they cannot sleep and from neighbours who claim a reduction in their rates. Policemen, however, seem impervious to the howling of unhappy dogs and the occasional "shurrup" seems to achieve great things. One of the more important tasks of a police cadet is to take the captive animals for walkies and sometimes these youngsters are advised to 'let the dog escape', and to write up the books as 'dog escaped'.

Unclaimed dogs are destroyed after seven days so this ruse saves the lives of many. The escape procedure, highly unofficial though it is, solves a lot of other problems because stray dogs very often find their own way home, having never been a true stray in the first place, but having been incarcerated through the misplaced kindness of an animal-lover. Someone else might find the 'escaped' dog and be willing to retain it until the true owner turns up, or indeed to retain it for ever. Not many come back a second time, which proves the sense of this procedure. It is somewhat embarrassing, however, when the same person finds the same dog two or three times a day and insists on fetching it back into custody, even though his kindness can lead to the death of a very nice dog.

On one occasion, I was on office duty from 2 pm until 10 pm at Eltering when a minute and elderly gentleman wearing plus fours and brogue shoes entered the police office. He was carrying a tiny Yorkshire terrier and it would be around 2.30 in the afternoon. The dog was one of the miniature variety which shiver all the time, and this one wore a blue ribbon in its hair. It wore a collar but bore no name and address. Its tiny eyes looked around in horror as the gentleman placed it on the counter and said, "I've just found it wandering in Flatts Lane, lost."

"Lost?" I commented. "Are you sure?"

"Aye, dogs like this don't wander alone, they're pets."

"There was no one about, eh?"

"No, Officer. No one. It's criminal, letting dogs like this wander at large. All kinds of harm could be done."

The little man steadfastly refused to take the dog home with him, which meant it had to be lodged in the dog house at Eltering Police Station, pending the arrival of its owner. Like all strays, if it was not claimed within seven days, it would have to be destroyed. In practice, we tried to save good dogs by dropping a word in the ear of the local newspaper reporter in the hope he would print a sob story in his columns. Very often, strays were handed over to people who would love and care for them, and many have acquired beautiful dogs through this system. It saved the Force, and ultimately the ratepayer, the cost of destroying the animals. I could hardly let this one escape – where would it run to?

The dog house at Eltering police office was a huge one. It had been built from plans prepared by the County Architect who probably thought he was designing a buffalo cage for the local zoo. The kennel was well constructed, airy and clean, and could have accommodated something as large as a buffalo. This little Yorkshire terrier was destined to be its first occupant and after I had entered the necessary details and description in the Stray Dogs Register, I carried it through the office and out into the yard where I placed it in the brand new dog house. It stood and shivered in the centre of the huge compound, its beautiful fringed eyes pitifully gazing up at me. I wondered if it slept on a silken bed at home. It yapped despairingly as I left, but once I was back in the office, its high-pitched protestations were beyond my ears.

I made sure we had sufficient food for it; we kept a stock of dog biscuits and were allowed to purchase other forms of dog food if necessary, the cost being recovered from the owner or from the person who decided to accept the dog as a stray, with our compliments. I popped out to see the little creature after about half-an-hour, taking with me a bowl of fresh water and some biscuits. It yapped its thanks, gazing expectantly at the wire netting.

I was surprised that no one had come to claim the little animal; pets like this were seldom lost and if they did go astray, you could guarantee their owners would come rushing around to claim them within a very short time. But not so with this little dog. By tea-time, no one had called or telephoned and I began to grow concerned about its future.

At five o'clock, another problem presented itself. A little girl entered the office towing a donkey behind her. She was about ten years old and had found it wandering down the lane behind her house. Her dad had instructed her to take it to the police station, with orders not to fetch it back. I noted her name and address and suggested she take it home until the owner was traced.

"My dad says you must keep it," she said firmly. "We've nowhere, we only live in a little house."

"Surely your dad knows somebody with a field," I suggested, knowing there was no formal procedure for dealing with found donkeys.

"No, no one. That's why he said to bring it here."

It wasn't a very large donkey, but it was a genuine, living one nonetheless.

"We've no fields here," I said inanely, "and I can't leave the office to take it anywhere."

"I've got to get ready for Brownies," she smiled. "Bye".

And with that, she turned and hurried from the station, leaving the benign ass standing before the counter like a baleful drunk. It looked about its new quarters and began to walk around, trailing the rope which was attached to a hessian halter.

"Oh no!" I shouted at it. "You can't have the freedom of the station, you're coming with me."

Our commodious new dog house was the answer. It was cosy and certainly large enough. The County Architect had some sense after all. Because the donkey might stand on the little dog, I decided to fetch the dog into the office, at least for the time being. And so the animals changed places. The donkey entered the dog house quite happily and sniffed at the clean hay, while the dog pranced and yapped in its new freedom. It followed me back into the office where it continued to yap and bark with delight. Because it was my meal time, I made sure all the doors were closed and allowed it the run of the place while I settled down to eat my sandwiches.

I was the only man on duty, consequently there was no one to relieve me. This meant I had to eat my meal at the counter. I didn't mind – there was nowhere else in the station, other than the cells, and this place was cosy enough. Besides, I now had an interesting little companion. I ate my sandwiches and dropped crumbs for it. Having discovered it liked cheese and chocolate icing, I named it 'Topsie' and we had a long and earnest conversation over our meal. It was an engaging little creature and I grew fond of it.

At six o'clock, a rough looking character pushed open the door and demanded, "Where's my donkey then?"

"Your donkey?"

"Aye, I heard tell it was here."

"There is a donkey here," I confirmed. "What's yours like?"

"Like? It's like any other donkey. Donkeys is all alike."

"You'll have to sign for it," I smiled, pointing to a place in the Found Property Register. "Received, one donkey in good condition."

"Where is it then?"

"In the stable out at the back," I said. I daren't say 'kennel'. "I'll fetch it through. How did it get lost?"

"Just bought it," he said. "For the kids. Some idiot left the gate open and it got out. Been missing since three o'clock, it has. I heard a little girl had fetched it in."

I couldn't bring to mind any offence of suffering a donkey to wander at large in a public place, so I led the man, whose name was Joseph Purvis, through to the dog-house-cum-stable. There he saw his pride and joy. His bland face beamed with open pleasure as he led his beast out of its cell and through the police station.

"Thanks," he said, and I was surprised to see him stuff a pound note into a charity collection box on the counter. He asked for the little girl's name too, and I gave it willingly. She was in for a tip as well. I held open the doors and he took his donkey outside where a small Morris pick-up was waiting. A plank reached the ground from the rear and the donkey climbed this quite happily, and allowed itself to be tethered to a hook on the rear of the cab. The van set off and the donkey seemed to enjoy the ride.

I decided to leave Topsie in the office because she was good company, but Sergeant Blaketon had other ideas. He arrived about seven-thirty to check that everything was in order, and noticed the shivering mass of blue-ribboned hair in the hearth.

"What's that?" he pointed at Topsie.

"Found property," I replied.

"What is it? A muff?"

"A dog, Sergeant," and I told him the story.

"Dogs is for the dog house, Rhea. Dogs must not be kept in offices. There is a Standing Order about that. That's what dog houses is for, Rhea. Dogs. And we've just had an architect-designed dog house built here. So put that animal where it belongs, lad."

"Yes, Sergeant."

Somewhat reluctantly, I carried Topsie outside and lodged her, unprotesting, back in the dog house. She looked very sad, I must admit, and I was sure she was crying as I closed the wire mesh door and turned my back upon her. She whimpered softly as I walked away.

In the office, Sergeant Blaketon was examining all the books and as I entered through the rear door, a tall, rather haughty woman entered through the front. Blaketon saw her and stood upright, revealing the full splendour of his ex-guardsman figure.

"Good evening, madam," he spoke politely.

"Sergeant," she said without smiling "I need help."

"Certainly, madam."

She was clearly a discerning person because she addressed herself to the sergeant, the senior officer present.

"Sergeant, I am the Honourable Mrs Allerston," she announced, "and I live near Scarborough. I have been visiting a sick relative in Leeds and I left my little dog with some nieces here in Eltering. They don't allow dogs in the hospital, you see, and I didn't like leaving her alone in the car. So I left her with relations. I have just returned to learn they have lost my dear Susie. My dear, dear little dog. She's a Yorkshire terrier, Sergeant. They have searched everywhere, everywhere. And all to no avail," the lady's voice was beginning to crack and I could see she might lose control. "My dear little dog, so clever and well behaved. I have searched too, all over the streets and lanes, and there are such horrid people about. I cannot find her, Sergeant. I have to ask you – and your, er, gentleman here, if you could mount a search for her. With police dogs, maybe? They can follow scents, can't they?"

Blaketon looked at me and, to my surprise, winked mischievously. "Madam, we shall be only too pleased to help." He drew a pad of paper towards him and adopted a very serious attitude. "Now, perhaps you can describe your dog?"

"She's very small," began the Honourable Mrs Allerston, "and she has a long, dark coat with silky ears. She is five years old and has a blue ribbon tied in her hair, in a bow."

"Ah!" he beamed with benevolence. "Then I believe we can help you. We have a similar dog in our dog house at this very moment."

"Dog house?" she exclaimed. "My Susie in a dog house with all those other strays?"

"Madam," he drew himself to his full and impressive height. "This is no ordinary dog house. It is architect-designed, and it is brand new. It was installed only last week, and it is full of lovely fresh hay. If this dog is your Susie – as I believe it is – then she is the very first occupant."

That was perfectly true. She had been the *first* occupant, and the donkey had been the second. But I hadn't got around to telling him of the donkey, and he had not reached the Found Property Register during his routine inspection.

"That is all right then," she nodded towards me. "I presume this, er, dog house is well disinfected after each occupant? And I assume my Susie has been well fed and cared for during her stay with you."

"Madam," O.B. drew himself to his full height again. "We take great pride in the way we care for animals placed in our custody. That dog house is pine scented, and I will personally ensure that it is cleaned and disinfected to avoid diseases. But as your Susie is our very first guest, there is no problem. She entered a virgin dog house."

"My Susie is very delicate you see, and she must not be exposed to doggie diseases."

"Madam," he boomed. "I am sure your Susie has enjoyed her stay with us."

"And you fed her? You didn't answer that."

"Police Constable Rhea fed her, Mrs Allerston. He gave her only the best of food that we possess and he tells me she ate like a horse. Isn't that true, P.C. Rhea?"

"Perfectly, Sergeant," I entered the spirit of the moment. "She ate like a horse."

"That is most unlike my Susie. She has a very small appetite and is very particular about her food."

"It must have been all the exercise and fresh air she's had today," he continued. "Now, madam, if you would sign for her and pay the cost of her upkeep, she will be returned to you in good condition. The cost will be five shillings. P.C. Rhea will be making out the receipt as I escort you to our dog house."

She paid and I wrote out the necessary receipt. I did not go out with them, and he told me later what had happened.

He had led the superior woman to the impressive new dog house whereupon Susie had leapt and barked with happiness at the sight of her mistress. O.B. had unlocked the door and the Honourable Mrs Allerston had entered the structure to collect her prize. And then she had screamed in horror.

"Susie!" she had cried. "What have you been eating?"

The dog had yapped happily at the sound of her voice, and as the Honourable Mrs Allerston had emerged, ashen-faced, Blaketon had looked in.

The other occupant had done a whoopsie right in the centre of the floor, and the pile of donkey manure dwarfed the tiny dog. The Honourable Mrs Allerston did not wait for an explanation, but rushed from the station gently stroking her dog and talking to it in a very soothing manner.

"You poor, poor darling," she was cooing. "What did they give you to eat then? Was it awful? It must have been painful too."

Sergeant Blaketon saw the funny side of this tale and

brushed aside my apologies for not informing him of the donkey's stay in our showpiece. I recalled his words that Susie had eaten like a horse and I often wonder what that lady thought we had done to her little Susie.

* * * *

Superintendent Arnold, the Divisional Commander at Strensford, kept a nondescript dog, a true Heinz-57 variety type mongrel whose predominant colour was black. It was hairy and had one lop ear, but in spite of its uncertain background, it was a happy little dog upon which was bestowed much love and affection, especially by Mrs Arnold.

Jimbo, the dog in question, loved to accompany its master upon his many supervisory perambulations and in its undying attempts to achieve this happiness, it would frequently dash from the house in defiance of the Arnolds. Jimbo seemed to know when the Superintendent was about to take a duty stroll about town; he also knew his master did not like his presence during those spells of police work. Jimbo would therefore rush out of the house and lurk in dark corners, waiting for his master to emerge, and once the Superintendent had left the house *en route* to the office, Jimbo would secretly follow him at a safe distance. He would reveal himself only when it was too late to return him to the house and would then follow the Superintendent around the town, steadfastly refusing to return home. This caused intense embarrassment to Superintendent Arnold but it delighted the townsfolk, specially when the Superintendent tried to pretend the dog was not with him. The public considered that a full uniformed police superintendent faithfully attended by a disobedient and scruffy mongrel was something of a prize sight.

I was drafted into Strensford for a period of night duty when the town was suffering from one of its regular and acute shortages of men. Because I was not too familiar with the town and its maze of alleys and back streets, I was allocated office duty for the duration of my night shift. It was an old police station of decidedly Victorian origin, and the office in question was an elongated room with a wooden partition running its length at one side.

The partition created a corridor for the public, and they told their tales of woe through a little window which had been built into it. On the inside of the window a counter ran the length of the partition. It had a sloping top formed by lots of desk lids. The space beneath the high counter was enough to accommodate the lofty stools and long legs of the policemen who sat there to minister to the public and to listen to their tales of human misery. The desks accommodated their paper work.

At the left-hand end of the wooden corridor was the entrance to Superintendent Arnold's office. Whenever he was supervising the night shift, he would stalk majestically along the corridor, poke his head around the end of the wooden partition and ask, "Anything doing?"

I was perched on one of those tall stools at eleven o'clock that night when I heard the unmistakable footsteps of an approaching policeman. He was heading towards the office. I waited and saw a figure pass the hatch and then the solemn features of Superintendent Arnold peered around the end of the partition and asked, "Anything doing?"

"No, sir, all quiet," I gave the traditional response, but he didn't withdraw his head. His eyes were glued upon something beneath the counter, something just beyond me. I looked down. There, lying blissfully asleep in the corner, almost out of sight, was a little black dog.

"That bloody dog!" he snapped. "It's followed me down again!"

At that time, I did not know of his perpetual battle with his dog, and merely said, "Really, sir?"

"You're not one of the regular constables, are you?"

"No, sir. I'm P.C. Rhea from Aidensfield, helping out."

"Ah, well, that dog is a bloody nuisance, Rhea. It persists in following me around the town, and dodges out of the house when it knows I'm on the way down here. It will follow me all around the town now, most embarrassing. It must be taught a lesson, once and for all. It must be taught that it must not follow me out of the house and it must not follow me around the streets."

And with that, he strode into the office, sailed right past me and seized the dog's collar. He hauled it towards his office.

The little dog, awake by this time and somewhat bewildered by this sudden turn of events, planted its feet firmly upon the wooden floor and refused to move. But Superintendent Arnold was a strong man. Gritting his teeth, he tugged and pulled the stubborn animal towards his office and eventually reached the door. He dragged the whimpering dog inside and slammed the door behind them. The dog was then subjected to what we might call the 'carpet treatment' – in other words, it was given a severe telling off.

But its treatment did not end there. There followed the distinctive sounds of someone beating the dog. The Superintendent's voice was admonishing it very loudly and very clearly, and his words were accompanied by the unmistakable sounds of a severe thrashing. The dog was howling loudly and this continued for what seemed an age, but in reality it was only a few minutes.

Finally, the door of Superintendent Arnold's office burst open and the pathetic figure of the little dog was hurled through the air to land near my feet. It wore a highly surprised look upon its tatty face, and its long black hair was considerably ruffled.

The Superintendent also looked ruffled.

"That isn't my dog, P.C. Rhea," he said, blushing furiously as he shrank back into his office.

It wasn't. This one belonged to a local sergeant. Arnold's own dog was still at home, sleeping soundly.

*   *   *   *

Claude Jeremiah Greengrass was always in trouble with the police. He had a formidable list of petty convictions, most of them acquired through blissful ignorance and carelessness, rather than by evil intentions. He was not a criminal in the strict sense of the word. He was just a bloody nuisance.

A small, pinched sort of man, he looked like an elf or an ex-jockey, and lived alone at Elsinby. He was brown-skinned due to a life in the open air, and earned his living in what I considered a dubious manner. He had no job, and performed small services for anyone who would pay. He gardened, washed cars, painted and decorated and cleaned out stables.

Everyone liked him, but no one trusted him. He was certainly light-fingered as his convictions testified.

Claude Jeremiah had a lurcher called Alfred. He had
acquired this poacher's friend from a pal who had gone to live
in the city. Claude Jeremiah had really done it as a favour,
but nonetheless, took his duties and responsibilities very
seriously. He set about training Alfred to the standard required of a domestic dog. He wanted him to stay, sit, heel and
lie instantly at his word of command.

To accomplish this part of Alfred's training, he took him
for long walks in quiet places where man and dog could
become deeply acquainted with one another without the
minor distractions of everyday life.

In Maddleskirk Wood, there is a small lake. A footpath runs
around its shores and a number of cottages overlook the path.
For Claude Jeremiah and Alfred, the place offered untold
possibilities. It offered more for Alfred than it did for his
master, for the area was full of scents, sounds and interesting
creatures. It was while walking along that path that the
trouble began.

Claude Jeremiah told me how Alfred had started to crawl
through a hole in the hedge and how he refused to return in
spite of his master's shouted commands. By the time Claude
Jeremiah had reached the point, Alfred had gone through the
hedge and there were the sounds of alarmed twittering from
behind the shrubbery. The twittering burst into panic-
stricken cries accompanied by the urgent flapping of many
wings.

Claude Jeremiah had located a garden gate and had
rushed through to find Alfred inside an aviary, thoroughly
enjoying himself as he chased hundreds of budgerigars. The
budgies weren't very happy about it, however, because Alfred
ran, barked and jumped among them, causing them to crash
against the wire netting in pathetic attempts to escape the
excited dog.

One fell to the ground and Alfred seized it in his mouth,
gripping it tightly and viciously shaking the poor creature just
as the irate owner rushed from his house. Claude Jeremiah
was, in the meantime, seeking an entrance to the enclosed
area but found none, and suddenly found himself staring into

the florid and angry face of a large, powerful budgie breeder. He had begun to apologise, but the man had said, "He's killed one and look at all the others! Battered, bruised and terrified out of their minds! All my years of work . . . " and the upset breeder was fitting a key into the lock of the door of his aviary as Claude Jeremiah shouted, "Sit, heel, lie down," all to no avail.

Once inside the cage, he cornered Alfred and after removing the dead budgie from his mouth, began to beat the wilful dog.

"I'll pay," he had said.

"You will that!" the angry fellow had shouted, looking around at the discarded feathers which still floated in the air. "Get yourself and that bloody animal out of here before it does any more harm. It'll take ages for them to settle down. And give me that dead one."

"He got in through a hole in the hedge," Claude Jeremiah had bleated, pointing to the hole in the netting.

"Your bloody dog made it bigger, didn't it?" the man had yelled. "Anyroad, my missus has called the police. They'll be here soon. You'll go to court over this, mister, you can tell your excuses to the police."

It was shortly afterwards that I entered the drama. I examined the scene and paid close attention to the hole used by Alfred. The aviary wall was in direct contact with the hedge; Alfred must have nosed his way through the hedge and forced his bulk through a hole in the netting, to find himself in the middle of the unsuspecting flock. And then he'd made the most of it. There's no doubt he enjoyed those minutes of action.

I took possession of the dead budgerigar for evidence of the crime and informed Claude Jeremiah that he would be reported for summons. His offence was allowing a dog to worry livestock on agricultural land.

When he appeared before the court, he pleaded not guilty. Claude Jeremiah always pleaded not guilty, no matter how the evidence was stacked against him.

The bench, chaired by Alderman Fazakerly, and comprising Mrs Pinkerton and Mr Smithers, listened as Sergeant Blaketon outlined the alleged facts and presented the case for the prosecution. The budgie breeder was first to give evidence and related how he'd found Alfred chasing his flock. He'd witnessed the death of one of his birds and had been present when the defendant admitted ownership of the lurcher in question. He valued the dead budgie at £2 0s. 0d.

I was next and told the court that, acting upon information received, I had visited Pond Cottage and had been shown the dead body of a budgerigar. It was within a wire-enclosed aviary, the floor of which was covered with feathers. Upon making an inspection of the walls, I had located a hole which led through the garden hedge and onto the footpath beyond.

I told their Worships how I had interviewed the defendant who admitted ownership of the dog. Upon being told he'd be reported for allowing his dog to worry livestock, the defendant had replied, "Livestock? A budgie isn't livestock – you can't get me for that one, P.C. Rhea." This response was duly noted by the magistrates.

Greengrass went into the witness box, took the oath and gave his version of the incident. He maintained the breeder should have known about the hole – there must have been a small one at least, and he accepted that Alfred had probably enlarged it. But, as he told the court, he felt the term *livestock* did not include budgerigars. The law was to prevent dogs chasing cows, sheep and other domestic animals.

When Greengrass stepped from the witness box, the Chairman sought the advice of his clerk, Mr Whimp.

"Is the fellow right, Mr Whimp?"

Whimp, as efficient as ever, had the necessary information to hand.

"The term is defined in the Dogs (Protection of Livestock) Act 1953, Your Worships. It means cattle, sheep, goats, swine, horses and poultry. Poultry is further defined as meaning domestic fowls, turkeys, geese and ducks."

"There is no mention of budgerigars?" asked the Chairman.

"None, sir."

"Could we include them within the term *domestic fowl*?" he asked.

"That is a matter for the court to decide," Mr Whimp smiled graciously at the assembled members of the bench.

"Damn it all, man," I heard the Chairman whisper. "There must be some guidance on this. What about domestic pigeons? Hasn't anyone had his pigeons worried by dogs? Or penguins at a zoo?"

"I recall one case, Your Worships, where hand-reared pheasants were regarded as livestock, but only during their captivity. There was another instance where doves were held to be *domestic fowls.*"

"Doves, eh?"

"Those cases were not reported, sir. The decision is yours, I'm afraid."

"Hrrumph. I suppose we are all right about the *agricultural land* bit?"

"That term includes allotments, orchards, arable, meadow or grazing land, sir."

"But not aviaries?"

"They are not specifically mentioned, Your Worships, although they may be part of a meadow, orchard or allotment, of course."

"Thank you, Mr Whimp."

In a judicial huddle, the magistrates concluded that the case was unsatisfactory from two standpoints. Alderman Fazakerly addressed the court and the accused.

"Claude Jeremiah Greengrass. The court has very carefully considered this case and feels that budgerigars are not livestock within the meaning of the Dogs (Protection of Livestock) Act. Furthermore, there is some doubt as to whether an aviary can be classified as agricultural land. The case is therefore dismissed. You are free to leave the court."

The breeder jumped to his feet. "What about my compensation?"

"That is no longer a matter for this court," Alderman Fazakerly spoke with an air of finality.

After the hearing, Sergeant Blaketon said to me, "We slipped up, Rhea. We should have taken him for failing to keep a dangerous dog under control, and sought a court order upon him to keep the lurcher under control. That can include anything done by dogs. I thought we were taking a risk with a worrying charge."

"He'll come again, Sergeant," I smiled with confidence.

"Besides, he's really done that breeder a good turn. All his budgies could have escaped through that hole, once they'd found it. As things are, he's only lost one."

"And will you tell him that?" smiled Blaketon.

*   *   *   *

Of the dogs which wandered around Aidensfield, the one which caused the most upset was an Alsatian called Emperor. It belonged to a gentleman called Hubert Fishburn who lived in a new bungalow and who was an "off com'd 'un", i.e. a newcomer to the community. Fishburn worked in York and from what I gathered during casual chats, he was something to do with insurance and worked in a managerial capacity. The tiny patch of land surrounding his miniature home was barely sufficient to keep a hamster, let alone a large Alsatian, so his agile and intelligent pet would take every opportunity to go for walks without waiting for his master.

I had spoken to Fishburn many times about Emperor and he was always most apologetic, usually blaming his wife and two small sons for the freedom enjoyed by the dog. In point of fact, it was not a great nuisance to the community of Aidensfield, but only to one poor old man. Unlike the musician's dog which loved dustbins, this one had only one passion, and that was the garden of a dear old character called Stumpy Sykes.

Stumpy had not worked for years because of leg trouble and coped admirably with his artificial leg. He spent his time in his garden which was superb by anyone's standard, and he earned a living of sorts by doing all kinds of odd jobs around Aidensfield. If anyone wanted a washer on a tap, a plug fitting to a kettle, a plot of land digging, a car washed or a kitchen painted, then Stumpy was their man. He was tall and lithe with thin black hair and a figure as slender as a child's. His teeth were brown with nicotine, but his eyes were piercing blue, sharp and alert. He was not married and, to my knowledge, never had been but lived in a delightful cottage which sparkled like new. It was a showpiece and was located in the older part of Aidensfield, being frequently photographed by visitors.

His garden was his pride and joy and in addition to

growing prize chrysanthemums and dahlias, he grew vegetables which he sold and flowers which he would fashion into
wreaths and posies.

Another of his talents was his ability to cure animals. In
this, he had a wide reputation and his secret was a large
brown pill, about the size of a walnut. He would shove that
thing down the throat of any sick dog, horse, pig, goat or
sheep and it always seemed to work. What it contained was a
mystery to me, but it never failed. He also cured smaller
creatures like cats, mice and hamsters, and even cage birds. In
short, Stumpy was a fascinating village character and a
stalwart of Aidensfield.

It was very unfortunate that Fishburn's Alsatian selected
Stumpy's garden for its daily visit. It would jump across the
wall and wander around Stumpy's plants, knocking them
down and destroying many in its tour of the garden, and then
it would leave its trademark in what was often a very obvious
place, like the centre of his beautiful lawn. After many
unsuccessful pleadings with Fishburn, Stumpy asked me to
talk to him.

I did, but it wasn't any good. Try as we might, that
Alsatian returned time and time again, and always to the
same place with the same smelly result. It can be argued that
it is no duty of a police officer to stop dogs fouling rose
gardens, but in a village the local constable must do all in his
power to keep the peace. I could see that this had all the
makings of a future breach of the peace. But the dog beat me.
Poor Stumpy grew desperate. The show season was practically at its height and although he loved animals, he began
to hate this one. But good will always triumph over evil, and
Stumpy did achieve his heart's desire. He stopped the dog
from entering his garden and he told me about it long after
the incident was over.

He knew the offending Alsatian came into his garden late
in the evenings, and as the early autumn began to draw its
cloak of darkness about the dale, the furtive visitations of the
dog were shrouded in gloom. Stumpy could sit at his bedroom
window and watch its arrival. He did this one night while
armed with a loaded shotgun. His love of animals compelled
him not to load the gun with a conventional cartridge.

Instead, he loaded this weapon with a sand cartridge. It was full of sand instead of lead shot, and they are not difficult to make from ordinary cartridges.

The big dog had duly arrived to carry out its intended purpose and from his vantage point above his garden, Stumpy took aim. With a tremendous bang, and at very close range, the gun was discharged and a wave of fast-moving sand hit the dog. It ripped every shred of fur from its hind quarters, leaving the front half of Emperor covered with normal hair but the rear was totally bare, like a plucked chicken. The dog howled in pain and surprise as it galloped home, its nudity embarrassing to behold.

Hubert Fishburn's surprise was total. He had no idea what had happened to his dog and he did not come to me. However he did go to see Stumpy, but only because Stumpy was the acknowledged expert on all animals and their ailments. Fishburn had no idea that Stumpy had caused Emperor's acute embarrassment. Stumpy had examined the dog.

"I reckon it sat in some lime," said Stumpy, seriously. "Up in them fields, you know, where they're liming t'land. Funny stuff is lime, it burns flesh and fur. I reckon your dog's done that, rolled in it, mebbe."

"Will it grow again?" asked Hubert.

"It might, with the right treatment," Stumpy advised him.

"You can treat it, can you?" There was a pleading tone in the man's voice.

"Aye, I reckon I can, but it'll cost you," said Stumpy, eyeing the anxious man.

"How much?"

"Depends," said Stumpy.

"On what?"

"On how long we've got to continue the treatment."

"But how much? I mean, do I pay per visit, or for the stuff you use, or what?"

"Each visit, two pounds inclusive should do it. I reckon ten or twelve visits will see him all right."

"Starting tonight?"

"Aye, if you like, fetch him up to our house."

It seems that Fishburn had a terrible job coaxing the dog

through Stumpy's garden gate and into the shed at the rear, but as the owner held the dog by its head, Stumpy began to smooth a thick, greasy ointment across the barren areas. It took him about a quarter of an hour, and he accepted the two pounds, saying, "Come back next week, same time."

I had seen Hubert once or twice, coaxing the unwilling dog into Stumpy's shed, and was told part of the story at the time. I knew better than ask Stumpy at that stage, but the weekly visits continued and the hair began to grow.

Finally, Stumpy said, "There we are, Mr Fishburn. I reckon that'll do now. The new hair's coming along fine, and that dog'll be back to normal very soon. That growth has a few weeks to go yet before it's fully grown, but it'll come along nicely now. There's no bald patches. You don't need me any more. It'll grow thick and fine in its own good time."

"I don't know how to thank you, Mr Sykes, really I don't. That lime must have been strong stuff."

"You never see cows sitting in it," smiled Stumpy. "I should keep your dog away from it in future."

"Oh, I will. He doesn't seem very keen on going out alone."

"Doesn't he now? I reckon he's learned his lesson, eh?"

"I think so. Well, thank you for all you've done. I really am most grateful. I'm amazed that you knew what it was and how to treat it."

"A lifetime of experience, Mr Fishburn," said Stumpy, accepting the final two pounds. "A lifetime in the countryside and a close knowledge of all animals."

And so Hubert Fishburn went off very happily. One evening, I popped in for a chat with Stumpy and he told me this tale, laughing until the tears ran down his cheeks.

"Has it ever been back to your garden, Stumpy?" I asked, laughing with him.

"Never, Mr Rhea. It never comes near the place now."

"That stuff you used to make the hair grow – what was it?" I put to him.

"It would have grown without it, Mr Rhea, but I thought I'd make him pay for all the damage his dog has done to my flowers. I got over £20 out of him for my cure. That makes us just about square."

"All right," I persisted. "But what was the stuff you rubbed on that dog?"

"Well, Mr Rhea," he said cautiously, "You won't tell him, will you?"

"I promise," I wondered what was coming next.

"Well, you see, my sister came to stay with me a few years back, and she left a jar of that stuff that women plaster over their faces. Cold cream, I think they call it. I used that on his dog."

:

Six

If Sergeant Blaketon was tall, severe and somewhat humour-less, my other sergeant, Charlie Bairstow, was round and happy with a bubbling sense of humour. He was an older man and had been a policeman all his working life. His pleasant nature led him to adopt a very philosophical outlook on life. It was his belief that no one should be arrested unless there was absolutely no other way of dealing with him. Although he was a very good practical policeman and a first-class sergeant, he liked the easy life. His pink face wore a perpetual smile and his hair always seemed to have endured a very stiff breeze. Jolly was a word which would describe him.

He was on duty one Sunday morning when I had to perform a four-hour stint at Ashfordly. I had motor-cycled in from Aidensfield and was working in the tiny office when I heard his voice. It called from the Sergeants' Office.

"This one's for you," he shouted from his sanctum.

I looked out of the office window to see a tall, smart woman approaching. She walked stiffly along the footpath towards the front door and as she came into the building, Sergeant Bairstow vanished with remarkable agility through the back entrance and hurried into the garden. I wondered why.

But the woman was standing before me at the far side of the counter and smiling sweetly into my face. She had a very 'peaches and cream' complexion, nice brown eyes, smart grey hair and horn-rimmed glasses. She stood very erectly before me, wearing a hat of deep cherry-red with matching shoes and handbag. Her coat was obviously expensive and I got the impression she was wealthy and influential. She might even be a magistrate and would be about sixty years old.

"Good morning, madam," I greeted her.

"Good morning," she spoke very pleasantly with a refined accent. "You're new, aren't you?"

"Yes, madam. P.C. Rhea, stationed at Aidensfield."

"Ah, well," she began earnestly. "It's about that man who's been pestering me. I've been here before, you know, he's a real menace. I've got to keep coming here to ask for your help. Jackson is his name."

I pulled a scrap pad towards me and began to make notes.

"Jackson, eh?"

"Yes, he's been at it again, Officer. Annoying me. He's always annoying me, you see."

"Could I have your name and address please?" it was always wise to begin at the beginning.

"Miss Fraser. Josephine Fraser. I live at 43, Prince Terrace. I'm a retired office worker, young man. Now, can you please do something about Jackson?"

"What's he done, Miss Fraser?"

"Done? He's sprinkled blue washing-up power all over my staircase. And it's not the first time. He must be stopped. He goes on and on, doing things like that all the time. It gets everywhere – I paddle it into my carpet . . ."

"How did he get into your house?" I asked, wondering whether he'd broken in. Had I a housebreaker on my hands? An arrest, maybe?

"I don't know. I just don't know," and an anguished look appeared on her calm face. "But he gets in all the same. I can't keep him out."

"Where does he live?" was my next question.

"Next door to me, Number forty-one," she said. "What an awful neighbour."

"It is not our policy to become involved in domestic issues," I tried to explain. "Have you seen a solicitor about him? If you arranged for a solicitor's letter to be sent, asking him to cease his activities, you'd surely find he would stop."

"Stop? He would not, young man. I've tried everything, I can tell you. Everything," and her voice began to rise in volume and pitch. "I'm about at my wits' end, you know. Everything that is possible has been done and he still keeps pestering me. All I want is for you to have a sharp word with him, and I know he'll stop, at least for a while."

Charlie Bairstow had not returned from his urgent mission, so I asked to be excused for a second and went to seek him. I wanted to ask if we, as the local police, got ourselves involved in Miss Fraser's troubles which appeared to be nothing more than a very localised domestic dispute. But he'd vanished completely.

"I'll pop around later this morning and warn him off, Miss Fraser."

"I would be most grateful," and with that she turned on her smartly dressed heels and left the station.

Half an hour later, still with no sign of Bairstow, I locked the office and walked round to Prince Terrace. I found No. 43. It was smart and clean with a bow window, a glass-fronted door and neat curtains. It was evident that Miss Fraser was a decent-living woman. Next door, however, was not quite the same. No. 41 was almost derelict. I walked up the path, knocked on the rotting door of No. 41 and it slid open beneath the touch of my hand.

"Anyone in?" I shouted inside.

No reply. I knocked again and entered, loudly proclaiming my presence and asking if anyone was at home. The place was deserted; there was no furniture and it was riddled with dampness and rot. I wondered if the villainous Jackson was a tramp, sleeping rough in this place.

I made a detailed search of the house. Apart from a stray cat, it was empty and there were no indications of recent human habitation. When tramps live in a house, there is always something to reveal their presence, like dirty cups, rotting food, cigarette ends, the foul smell of unclean human-ity and so forth. But this place bore none of those signs. I left and decided to acquaint Miss Fraser with my action. It seemed that Jackson had left his address, possibly due to her threatened police action. I knocked on her door and it was opened almost immediately.

"Ah!" she beamed. "You're just in time for coffee. Would you like some, Officer?"

"I'd love one," I said and followed her inside. She kept a beautiful home, furnished with genuine antiques and interest-ing paintings. The carpets were thick and lush, the furniture of good quality and the decor of a very professional standard.

Everything in the house showed taste and discrimination. She led me into her beautiful lounge which overlooked the street where I noticed a tray already set with coffee and waiting on a low table. It bore a silver coffee-set, with delicate china cups. Two cups. And the coffee pot was steaming appetisingly.

Over coffee, she told me more about her running battle with Jackson. She agreed that today's visit to the police had terrified him, and he'd fled. That was her explanation of the empty house and I accepted it. But that was not all. Now she'd got a captive audience, she insisted on letting me know about his other activities. It seemed he would enter her house when she was out and move things around. He'd change the position of her ornaments, or tilt the pictures. He'd enter the bedroom too, and interfere with her clothing, hiding things so she couldn't find them. And, horror of horrors, he examined her underwear in the drawers and cupboards; she knew, because they'd been moved. He played drums at night and had sent swarms of invisible insects into her kitchen, where they'd contaminated the food. And then he sent rays through the walls, invisible rays which kept her awake at night and gave her bad dreams.

And as I sipped her delicious coffee from exquisite china cups, I realised she was crackers. She was clean, presentable, charming and well-spoken, but she was nuts. Judging by the house, she was comfortably off and money was not a problem. On the face of things, she was everything a favourite aunt might be. But she was as nutty as the proverbial fruit cake. I couldn't say whether she was batty enough to be certified, but she was certainly very odd.

It took me a long time to escape. She talked on and on about Jackson, regaling me with horrific tales about his interference with her life and his domination of her daily routine. When I began to ask specific questions, however, it transpired she had never seen him. She could give me no description at all. I wondered if he was a meths drinker or just a character who passed in the night. An hour and a half later, when eventually I managed to leave, I found Sergeant Bairstow back in his office. He smiled graciously as I entered.

"Well, Nicholas, did you kick Jackson out of that house?"

"Jackson!" I cried. "Who is that man? Why does he cause her so much trouble? I think she's imagining most of it."

"All of it," he said. "She imagines all of it. There is no Jackson; it's all in her mind. She's lonely, she likes male company and she's never had a feller. She's a frustrated virgin, Nick, and that's why she's like that. That's how they grow up when they're frustrated. She needs a bloody good man to sort her out, if you understand what I mean. Today, she's had a charming young man in for coffee and that will keep her going for a week or two. She'll go to bed with you, in her mind's eye that is, but she'll be back to see us, mark my words."

"You set me up for that one, didn't you?" I laughed.

"We always let the new lads deal with Miss Fraser, Nick, she loves them, you see. It gives her deep satisfaction – that's what we are here for, isn't it? To satisfy the public."

I gave a lot of thought to poor old Miss Fraser just in case I was on duty next time she called. As things worked out, I was on duty again at Ashfordly when she came to the station. It was about a month later.

"He's been at it again, Officer," she told me seriously. "Blue powder again."

"Not all over your stair carpet?" I cried.

"No, in the frying pan this time. All over my cooking utensils."

"I'll be around shortly to have words with him," I promised.

An hour later, I knocked on her door and she invited me in for coffee as before. I accepted because she was entertaining and the coffee was excellent. This time there were biscuits.

I told her I had dealt with Jackson once and for all. I told her he would never trouble her again, ever.

"What have you done with him?" she asked, her eyes wide with anticipation.

"I've arranged for a deportation order," I said seriously. "Jackson is to be deported to Australia. The order becomes effective at noon next Friday, when he will be transported to Australia. He sails from Southampton."

She did not speak for a long time. Then she smiled. "Thank you," she said. "Thank you very much."

"He'll never trouble you again," I assured her. I had no trouble leaving after imparting this news. She seemed numbed and I left her, having gained the impression that she was sad. Nothing happened for several weeks after that visit, and we saw nothing of her. Then an inspector from Eltering called me into his office.

"What the hell have you been up to, Rhea?" and he waved a letter at me.

"I've got this letter from the Home Office," he glared at me. "It concerns a complaint they've received from a Miss Fraser of Ashfordly and it has come to me via the Chief Constable. There's hell on in high places, Rhea."

I blushed deeply. I wasn't aware that I had done anything to justify a complaint, particularly one which involved the Home Office. I knew that the Home Secretary was responsible for all law and order in the country, so had I broken some golden rule?

"I didn't do anything wrong, sir," I said, not knowing the basis of her complaint.

"Do you know the rules about emigrating to Australia?" he asked. "They don't accept convicted criminals – if you have convictions for crime, you cannot begin a new life in Australia. They don't want convicts, not any more."

"I heard of something like that, sir. Isn't it connected with the ten-pound passage scheme?"

"Yes," he acknowledged, his face breaking into a smile. "It seems that you have arranged the deportation to Australia of a very dangerous criminal called Jackson. Miss Fraser is demanding an enquiry into the matter – she wants the Home Office to investigate the system which allows a notorious villain like Jackson to dodge the rules. How did he get through Customs? How did he evade the Special Branch? Why has Australia accepted him? The Home Office has asked the Chief Constable for a full report."

"It was like this, sir . . . " I stuttered.

"I don't want to know, lad! Just write the report, will you? I'm sure the Home Secretary will be very amused to know how you dealt with a man who puts blue powder into frying pans and who conjures up swarms of invisible insects from the air. But I think you had better arrange for the return of this man, Jackson, before we have a diplomatic incident."

"Yes, sir."

"You haven't got rid of him, have you, Rhea? You'll have to come up with another idea, won't you?"

"Yes, sir," and I crept away to write my report.

*   *   *   *

A few months later, I was subjected to another of Sergeant Bairstow's orders. Technically, the mission was no part of my duty; it was an extension of my role as village constable, but he considered it important enough to justify particular action on my part.

I received his phone call just after lunch one Friday when he updated me with the daily messages. Having concluded that essential part of the conversation, he said, almost in passing, "Oh, Nicholas, there's a little job for you. It's just off your beat, in Maddleskirk, but as you're out and about this afternoon, I thought you might do it."

"Willingly, Sergeant," I agreed, having forgotten about his disappearing trick when Miss Fraser called.

"It's a Mrs Dulcimer and she lives at Acorn House. Audrey Dulcimer."

"I've got that, Sergeant," I wrote down her name and address.

"She's had another of her confrontations with a policeman in York, and she must produce her driving licence and insurance certificate. It's a regular occurrence with her – she's always getting booked for parking or for obstruction in York, and she dislikes coming all the way into the office, merely to produce her documents. It means a special journey, so she gives me a ring and I ask someone to call around. It's not a special journey for you because you're out and about anyway. So pop in, lad, it's a courtesy job. I realise it's her responsibility to fetch in her papers, but we do try to oblige where possible, eh?"

"Yes, Sergeant."

"Good. Glad to know you'll co-operate. Be kind to her, she's a barrister's wife. Nice woman, good house. And I'm sure she'll give you a cup of tea as well."

"It'll be a pleasure, Sergeant."

"I know it will. Do you know the house?"

"No, but I'll find it."

"It's a big place just off the main street, there's white gates."

"I'll find it," I assured him.

"I said one of our men would be there about three-thirty? Does that fit in with your plans, Nicholas?"

"Fine," I said.

Having dealt with my paperwork, I mounted the trusty Francis Barnett and began my afternoon patrol. With just over an hour to use before my appointment with Mrs Dulcimer, I visited one or two farms to check their stock registers and popped into some local stores to warn against a confidence trickster who preyed on rural shopkeepers. His trick was to ask for cash in advance, on the pretext that he could supply goods at huge discounts. He'd conned a local off-licence into parting with £50 for cut-price whisky and had done a similar trick on an electrical goods shop, taking £40 on the understanding he'd deliver cut-price radio sets. We knew the goods would never arrive and were surprised at business-men parting so readily with their money to people they didn't know. It seemed that the opportunity to obtain something for nothing could be relied upon to make a man and his money easily part company. The possibility of gaining summat for nowt never fails to achieve results.

At twenty past three, I drove into Maddleskirk, a long sprawling village with rows of tiny houses, all built of mellow yellow stone with red pantile roofs. I drove slowly, seeking the double white gates of Acorn House and found them next to the church. I drove up the drive which twisted through rhododendron bushes and parked my machine on its stand outside the front door.

It was an impressive house, built in the style of the 1930s with attic windows and a double garage tucked behind the living quarters. The woodwork was pure white and the garden was a picture. The place bore an air of extreme efficiency, and had a colour supplement aura about it. I removed my crash helmet, rang the door bell and waited.

Soon I heard soft footsteps on the inside and the door

opened to reveal a very slender woman with greying hair and a ready smile. Her face was lightly made up, showing off her grey eyes, good teeth and fine skin. She was tall by feminine standards, probably around 5 feet 9 inches, and wore high-heeled shoes, a white pleated skirt and a light summery blouse, open at the neck. I couldn't estimate her age with any accuracy, but I'd say she was in her middle forties.

"Mrs Dulcimer?"

"Yes, do come in," she oozed. "I'm awfully sorry to drag you all this way, Officer, but your sergeant is so good, isn't he? He knows it means a special journey . . . "

"I was in the area," I lied easily. "It's of no consequence."

"I'm so pleased you could come. I always seem to get myself into trouble when I visit York. It's a driver's nightmare, isn't it? But do come in. You'll have a cup of tea?"

"Thank you," and I stepped inside. She suggested I hang the motor-cycling helmet on the hallstand, but I wore no other protective or waterproof gear because it was a fine summer day. I followed her into the lounge, allowed myself to be settled on her settee and flicked through a copy of *She* while she wafted into the kitchen to prepare the tea. I heard the kettle sing immediately; she had obviously been prepared. Moments later she returned bearing a tray and teapot, with cups, milk and sugar.

She settled at my side. I could smell the perfume as she leaned forward to pour two full cups, asking if I wanted sugar. I shook my head and accepted the cup from her. She chattered away very amiably and told of her motoring frustrations in York, the delights of living in the country, the benefits of this particular house and about her family. She had two sons, grown up and now at university. She prattled on about her boys, both studying law and destined to follow in father's legal footsteps. Mr Dulcimer, I learned, was a busy and successful barrister whose skills took him all over England, a task which meant he was often away from home. I enjoyed her tales; she was highly attractive and easy to converse with.

As our talk progressed, she confided in me, saying she had no money troubles and occupied herself with charity work, church duties and other essential village affairs. She did this to while away the time when her husband was absent, and to fill her lonely day-time hours. Having finished the tea, she went to a desk in the corner of the room and returned with a buff envelope.

"Insurance and driving licence," she handed me the envelope. "You'll find they are in order."

I examined them and wrote their data in my book. This was necessary because I had to transmit the details to the police officer who had stopped her in York. He would write to Ashfordly Police Station to request the information. I noted the number of the insurance certificate, its dates of validity, the registered number of her car, the conditions under which it was issued and the name of the issuing company. Similarly, I wrote down the details of her driving licence, noting that it was signed and that it was current.

"Fine," I said, pushing the documents back into the envelope. "All in order."

"With my husband being so involved with the law, I can't afford to take chances," she smiled. "More tea?"

"No thanks," I closed my notebook and slipped it back into my tunic pocket. "I'd better be going."

"Oh, must you?" she asked softly. "There's enough in the pot for another cup," and before I could refuse, she began to pour. I shrugged my shoulders in cheerful resignation and accepted the second cup. It tasted good, I must admit, and I found her a charming person. I could imagine her being the centre of attraction at any function, whether formal or informal, for her range of topics was remarkable. She seemed well read but soon she turned her attention to me. She asked about my growing family, my work and my impressions of this area, and it wasn't long before I realised she had steered the conversation around to her own home.

"We haven't been here long either," she was telling me, sipping delicately and smiling at me. "We had a house in York, then moved out to Stillington. We came here about five years ago. My husband likes this village – it's not so flat as York and we love the moors. They're so handy for walks, you know. We found this house quite by chance, motoring here one week-end, and it was just right for us. Spacious, detached and in very good order. We did a bit of work upon it, mainly on the interior, but the fabric was sound."

"It's a very nice house," and I told her how much I would like a house of that sort, when eventually I left the Force.

"Would you like a look around?" she asked pleasantly.

In all innocence, I said I would love to have a look around. She showed me the ground floor, the dining-room with its oak suite made by Mousey Thompson of Kilburn, the kitchen with its fabulous fitted range, the study with Mr Dulcimer's enviable law library and filing system, the veranda with its array of potted plants and the garden beyond. There I admired an ancient sun-dial, the goldfish pond and the crazy paving. To say it was beautiful was an understatement; it was worthy of inclusion in one of the Sunday colour supplements. She was a fortunate woman and I felt a twinge of envy as we returned to the lounge. I caught the occasional whiff of perfume as she walked close to me, sometimes very close.

"Would you like a look upstairs?" she ventured.

"Thank you," I said, with even more innocence. After a ground floor of such opulence and taste, what would the bedrooms be like?

She led me up the wide carpeted stairs, showed me the tiled bathroom with its pale green fittings and the shower unit in the corner, the boys' bedrooms, the guest room with its bathroom *en suite* and finally, her room. This was exquisite; the predominant colour was pink, with matching curtains, carpet and bedspread. I could sense she was excited, her voice trembled as we talked. She came very close to me.

"It's beautiful," I said with genuine feeling.

"Like me?" she cried and to my total astonishment, she literally threw herself onto the bed and in a single movement, flung her skirt across the room. She was naked beneath. From the waist down, she wore nothing at all as she lay on that gorgeous silken cover, smiling up at me.

But there are certain things that do not come within the scope of a policeman's duty, and that was one of them. I fled. In something of a daze, I returned to Ashfordly Police Station to enter the details of Mrs Dulcimer's documents in a register kept for the purpose. It took a long time because my mind was still reeling from this experience, or perhaps the lack of it! But we had been warned of women like this at Training

School, and all kinds of ghastly ends to one's career had been threatened if any of us succumbed. As I wrote the details in the register, Sergeant Bairstow entered the office.

"All correct, Sergeant," I trotted out the automatic response.

"Good," he returned. "Anything to report?"

"Nothing, Sergeant," I said.

"You, er, visited Mrs Dulcimer, did you?" he asked, his merry eyes watching me carefully. I noticed a definite twitch at the corners of his mouth, the beginnings of a smile, maybe?

"I did," I wondered if he knew what she was like.

"You found everything in order, did you?"

"Everything was in order, Sergeant," I realised what he was getting at, the crafty B! I decided to string him along for a while.

"Nice woman," he muttered eventually.

"Very pleasant," I was determined to continue this cat-and-mouse game for as long as possible. Dare I admit I hadn't accepted her generous offer? Or should I let him think I had? His questions told me he'd known what was in store for me, and I now realised why she wanted the policeman to visit her, in order to check her driving documents. How many had been there before me? Had he, I wonder?

"Alone, was she?" he continued.

"All alone, Sergeant. Nice house, too. A very nice woman," I said concluding my written entry with a flourish of my pen.

"Hmm," he walked about the small office, his chin cupped in his hand. "I'm pleased everything was in order."

"I'm glad I didn't have to book her for an offence," I said seriously. "She gave me a lovely cup of tea and besides, her husband is a barrister."

"Yes, he is, Nicholas. He's away a lot, they tell me."

"Yes, he's a busy man, and a prosperous one by the look of it."

There was another long pause.

"Did she show you round the house, Nicholas? She's very proud of it, they tell me."

"A nice place," I smiled at him. "They've done a fair bit to it, I believe, in the five years they've been there. It's beautifully situated, isn't it?"

"I've never been," he told me. "I've only heard, you know, from lads who've been up there, checking her credentials."

"It's the sort of place I'd love to own," I was thinking of the pittance that policemen earned.

I wondered how long he would question me in this oblique sort of way, so having completed the entry in the register, I closed the book, slipped it back onto its shelf and prepared to leave. He watched me and made small talk about nothing in particular, chattering merrily as I placed my helmet on my head.

"I'm going round by Briggsby, Sergeant," I told him as I started to walk from the office. "I've a call to make there – a youngster wants to join the police cadets. I'm seeing him after school."

"Cheerio, Nicholas, " he called as I walked out, and as the door had almost closed behind me, I heard him shout, "Did you get your oats then?"

I pretended not to hear his question. I simply waved a hand in reply, a farewell gesture as the door clicked home. I left him in blissful ignorance, which I reckoned was the best thing to do.

*   *   *   *

Another interesting encounter with the fair sex occurred when I was on early duty in Eltering. It was my duty to patrol the town's streets between 6 am and 10 am, due to a shortage of local manpower. Eltering is a small North Yorkshire market town located on the southern edge of the moors. It is therefore appropriately known as 'Gateway to the Moors' but it was never busy during those morning hours. The only regular indications of early morning work came with people like the milkman, the postman and window-cleaners.

As eight o'clock came around, the town grew more active. People began to move. Some emerged from their homes to catch the shops, to buy papers, cigarettes, milk or coffee, while the policeman spent that time wishing them all 'Good morning'. It was pleasant, watching the town come to life. In some sense, I enjoyed this duty. It differed greatly from my own rural heaven, but it could be very monotonous from time to time, particularly during the dark winter months. Summer brought a welcome cheeriness to the place, however, and it was a late July morning as I made this early morning patrol around the town, using streets not yet aired. The very early morning workers had left – the eight o'clockers hadn't yet emerged. I had the town to myself as the church clock struck seven.

I decided to patrol the Aislaby estate, a new housing complex on the western edge of this charming town. I knew I could walk up there, do a circuit of the streets on foot and be back in town for eight o'clock, in order to make my point on the hour outside the post office.

With my cape over my shoulder in case of rain, I set off. It was a pleasant stroll. There was nothing criminal to worry me, although I did check a few parked cars to see if their tax discs were displayed. I examined a few lock-up premises *en route*, to establish that no shopbreakers had paid illegal nocturnal visits. But all was in order. All was quiet, as I would report to any sergeant or inspector who might ask. Having performed that perambulation, I made my way back to the town centre, noting that it was about a quarter to eight. The morning bustle was beginning.

As I made my slow, methodic way down the gently sloping gradient into the town centre, I became aware of some urgent activity ahead of me. A policeman can sense when something is happening – people begin hurrying towards whatever it is. Everyone wants to see it, so they can talk with authority in the pubs, clubs and offices, and there is a tangible scent of excitement in the air. Those symptoms were happening in Eltering right now. Men were hurrying towards some unknown incident just out of my sight. Whatever it was, it had literally brought the town centre to a halt. There was a car with its driver's door standing open, a butcher running with his blue-and-white striped apron flapping about his knees, a milkman dashing along with a crate rattling at his side, a pedal cycle lying in the gutter, its rear wheel spinning uselessly.

And so, quite naturally, I speeded up my regulation pace. I began to hurry. I had no idea what had happened, but the chances were that it would involve the police. Unexpected incidents usually did. I simply followed the growing number of hurrying men. Where they came from, I will never know, although the clatter of closing doors, the abandoned cars, the shops standing empty and the number of early morning businessmen provided me with a good clue. Somehow, word of the incident had spread like wildfire.

Just around the corner, I found the main clutch of men. They were standing around the entrance to an alley just off the centre of the town, so I used my elbows to good advantage. I pushed my way to the front.

"What's going on?" I asked in what I hoped was a voice bearing some hint of authority.

A shirt-sleeved man answered. "It's a young woman," he grinned. "Starkers. Down there – she's told us to keep out."

"Down there?" I pointed down the alley. It was a narrow passage between a shop and an hotel, and it had a corner at the distant end. She'd gone around the corner, and I heard her shout.

"Don't any of you dare come down here, not one of you, or I'll scream."

"Who is she?" I asked of anyone who might answer.

"Dunno," one of them said. "She's bollock naked, Officer. Not a bloody stitch on. She was running down the street, crying."

"When?"

"Just now," he confirmed. "A few minutes ago. She bolted down there, like a scared rabbit."

"And you all ran after her, eh?"

"Cor. Not 'arf, Officer," grinned one of them. "I mean, it's not every morning a naked woman runs down the street, is it? Not in Eltering, any road."

"How old is she?" was my next question.

"Early twenties, mebbe. Beautiful too, lovely knockers on her."

"All right, lads," I tried to defuse the situation. "The fun's over. Imagine this was your own daughter or wife, eh? It might be, mightn't it? She'd be scared, wouldn't she? With a lot of sex-starved blokes chasing her through the streets."

They murmured something non-committal and there were lots of bawdy comments about running in the opposite direction if it had been the wife, but at least I had gained their attention. They refused to leave just yet, however. They wanted to have another look at her. I had to save this slip of a lass from a fate worse than death.

"Hello," I shouted down the passage. "I'm the policeman. It's P.C. Rhea from Aidensfield. You can't stay there all day – the town's coming to a standstill."

"I'm not moving. Tell them to go away."

"You can't go through the streets like that!" I called to her, although I'd not yet had the pleasure of viewing her body. "I've got a cape, you can put that around yourself. It will cover you up, and we can get you home."

There was a long pause, during which the assembled men began to make ribald remarks about my intentions, and then she said, "All right. Just you."

This was one of the perks of the job, and so with wolf whistles and calls of encouragement, I walked the few yards along the alley to meet her. She was cowering behind the corner of the wall, in the lee of a tiny outbuilding of some kind, and her bare arms did their best to cover her nakedness. She had sandy hair and a face covered with freckles, but her body was young and luscious. She wore no shoes – she hadn't a stitch on.

"I'm married," I said as if that made any difference and with a flourish, I removed my cape from my shoulder. "Here," I offered it to her. "Try this for size."

With a weak smile, she opened it and draped it about her body. It came down to her knees. If she walked through the street wearing it, no one would know she was naked beneath. At this time of day, comparatively few people were about anyway – all those who were abroad were, at this minute, swarming around the exit of this alley.

"All right," I shouted at the waiting voyeurs. "The show's over, lads. She's covered up now. Off you go and let the lady through."

One or two of them drifted back to their jobs or morning chores, but the inevitable handful remained.

"Can you face them?" I asked her.

She nodded.

"Come on," I took her arm, holding it through the folds of the cape, and led her from the passage. A cheer went up from the assembled crowd and she blushed furiously, although recognising the good-humoured affection behind their noise. They drifted away as I accompanied her through the streets, using the quieter routes.

Once the initial audience had dispersed, no one paid any attention to us. The sight of a girl in a long cloak was not unusual, nor was it odd that a policeman should walk along the street chatting to a local person. By the time we reached her home, she was quite affable.

"Well?" I asked eventually. "What was all that about?"

She smiled. "Sex," she said. "I wouldn't let him, so he threw me out. The door's got a Yale lock and it clicked behind me. I couldn't get back in. I was crying and I panicked."

"Where?"

"Just round the corner from here," she pointed. "Up one of those alleys."

"Why run right through the town?" I asked.

"I've a friend down there," she said. "Janice. A good pal. I thought she'd let me in."

"But at eight o'clock in the morning? With the town just getting busy?"

"I didn't know it was eight o'clock" She laughed now. "I thought it was about five, and it wouldn't be busy."

"So what happens now?" I asked her.

"I'll go home. I'll show you where I live and then you can have your cape back."

"I thought you said it was along one of these alleys?"

"That's where I was last night, with this feller. I don't live there, I live further along."

"Boyfriend?" I asked.

"Sort of," she nodded. "He went crazy, honest, when I said no. I got out of bed and said I was going home, so he kicked me out. Pushed me downstairs and out of the door."

"What will your mother say when you turn up like this?"

"It's not my mother I'm worried about," she said frankly "It's my husband!"

"Husband?" I cried.

"Yeh, luckily he's away at sea. I hope he doesn't find out or he'll kill me."

"I won't tell him," I promised her.

We reached her house, a small cottage just off a side street near the Co-op, and I had to force a window with my pocket knife, because her key was at the other place, in her clothes. I managed to open a window, climbed inside and released her latch to let her into her own house.

"Thanks," she breathed, and thereupon removed my cape. She stood before me unashamed and proud, smiling at me. She asked, "Are you staying a while?"

"No," I had to say. "Duty calls."

"I think you policemen are wonderful," she winked at me, closing the door as I left. "Do call again, won't you?"

"I might," I said, knowing full well that I wouldn't go near the place. It would be several weeks later when I was patrolling the town during the evening. A pretty young woman stopped me outside the chip shop, offered me a chip and said, "Hello".

"Hello," I said, accepting the chip but not recognising her.

"You don't remember me, do you?" she smiled. "I'm all dressed up now."

"Ah!" I realised who it was. "Sorry, I didn't recognise you with your clothes on. You've had a new hair-do too?"

"You are observant," she grinned, offering me another chip. I accepted her chips, and learned her first name was Sylvia.

*   *   *   *

"I must stress that this is an informal chat at this stage, P.C. Rhea," said the Superintendent. "It might lead to an official complaint against the police, however. I am anxious to hear your side of the story."

"Yes, sir." I was in the Superintendent's office at Divisional Headquarters, wondering what was coming next. He lifted a file from his desk.

"This," he said, "is a complaint against you."

I'd always regarded myself as the epitome of good behaviour, and I was shaken by this revelation. I knew that a lot of police officers welcomed complaints about their men because it proved they were doing their job. But that didn't take into account the mental anguish when one heard a complaint about oneself.

"Do you know a Miss Angela Hamilton in your village?" he asked.

"Yes, sir. She's a big chapel woman, a do-gooder and all that. She's very pleasant – in her early forties, sir. A bit prim and proper maybe, if you know what I mean."

"I sensed that from her letter. Now listen. She accuses you of infidelity. She has been observing your movements, P.C. Rhea, and alleges that you, a family man and father of three children, have been visiting some of the ladies of the village at late hours. Miss Hamilton has a record of those dates and times. Your police motor-cycle has been seen in close proximity to their homes – there's a widow called Mrs Christian, a young blonde called Kay who hasn't been in the village for long, a woman whose husband goes away on business for long periods, and several others. All, according to Miss Hamilton, are ladies of doubtful virtue."

"Oh?" I replied. This latter snippet was news to me. They were all nice women, so far as I knew.

"Is that all you've got to say?" he asked me.

"There's not much more I can say, sir, because my motor-cycle will have been near or right outside everyone's house at some time or other. How long has this supposed orgy been going on?"

"Over the past four or five months."

"I can't remember all my movements, sir," I said honestly. "Damn it all, I've kept observations in the village, I've made crime enquiries, I've renewed firearms certificates and done a host of other jobs which entail visiting other people's homes at all hours."

"I am sure there is a perfectly logical explanation, P.C. Rhea, so I want to hear your story before I decide whether or not to take official action. But remember I've got this written complaint about the conduct of one of my men, and it must therefore be investigated. I'll supply you with the alleged dates and I want you to go home and explain, in writing, the presence of your motor-cycle outside those places at the material times. Go home and write up your report, and I'll decide what further action to take."

I told Mary all about it. Being a good wife, she sympathised and affirmed her trust in me, whereupon I adjourned to my office to find all my old pocket books. I now had the chore of checking every date mentioned in Miss Hamilton's letter.

"She's in the ideal position to spy on people, living right in the middle of the village," Mary observed. "And her a pillar of the chapel! Fancy spreading malicious rumours like that! I've a good mind to go and tell her what I'd like to do with her!"

"Hold on, girl, that would only make matters worse. Let's find out why I was at those houses, and why my motor-bike was around at the times she mentions."

It wasn't a long job to unearth the information because my pocket books told all. For each of the dates provided in Miss Hamilton's accusation, there was a true explanation – crime prevention advice to the young widow; Kay Hartford, the blonde newcomer, had a firearm certificate for variation, and the wife whose husband was away on business had twice found footprints in her garden and wanted police action. I had kept observations on her garden from another building and from time to time, called to acquaint her with my action to stop prowlers. And so it went on until I had a complete answer to all her charges.

I typed these into a full report and submitted it to the Superintendent.

"Thank you, P.C. Rhea, for your co-operation," the big man said. "I'll drive out to have a word with this woman myself. She's a mischief-maker."

But his action did not stop her.

The bishop of the Anglican diocese received a complaint from Miss Hamilton, who had reported that the vicar's estate car had been seen outside certain ladies' homes at strange hours. This resulted in the vicar being called to the bishop's palace for a down-to-earth chat. Similarly, it seemed the postman had been dallying too long at specified calling places and the Co-op van driver seemingly spent too long upon his deliveries.

The Head Postmaster of the area and the manager of the Co-op duly received letters from Miss Hamilton. As things

tend to happen upon such occasions, it wasn't long before the
Co-op driver happened to mention this to the postman, who
in turn laughed about it as he talked to me. I thus became
aware of the whole story. It didn't take much intelligence to
realise that the complaints from the frustrated Miss Hamilton
were all levelled against men in the public eye. The same
ladies featured in all her letters. Invariably, they were attractive women. It was therefore in the course of my duty that I
popped in to see the vicar, the Reverend Clifton, to ask about
his chat with the bishop. His bishop, it transpired, had been
most uncharitable about it, apparently more concerned about
the tarnished image of the church than the personal dilemma
of his vicar.

"She's a member of the chapel flock, isn't she?" I put to the
vicar.

"Happily, she's not one of mine," laughed Roger Clifton.
"I might have a word with her minister. She's got to be
stopped."

"I think I could stop her," I suggested.

"You really think so?" beamed Roger Clifton. "I'd be most
grateful if you could. How would you tackle the job?"

I said I'd prefer to be non-committal at this stage, and said
I'd like to have a word with the minister of the chapel first. A
lot depended upon his co-operation. After speaking at length
with the minister, Pastor Smith, I next discussed my idea with
the postman, the Co-op van driver and finally, the Reverend
Roger Clifton. I told him how pleased they all were and he
felt it was a sound suggestion.

A few weeks later, Miss Angela Hamilton found herself
being summoned to the presence of Pastor Smith and the
elders of her local chapel, all sitting in stony silence.

"Miss Hamilton," coughed the minister solemnly as she
settled before them. "You enjoy a high position within this
chapel, but I am afraid I have had a series of complaints
about your behaviour."

"About me?" she cried.

"I have a list of dates and times when motor-vehicles
belonging to certain men of this village have been seen
outside your house at some very strange hours. Indeed, some
have been noted outside your house for lengthy periods

during the day. I need mention only the postman, the Co-op van, the policeman's motor-cycle . . . Now, Miss Hamilton, I know you are an unmarried lady, and I am not suggesting for one minute that you are leading an immoral life, but for a lady in your position, as warden of our chapel . . ."

When Pastor Smith told me of this chat with her, he said that it was at that stage of his conversation, that Miss Hamilton had ceased to listen. The frown of concern upon her face had become a quiet smile of success.

But she didn't write any more letters to my Superintendent.

Seven

The atmosphere at the Hopbind Inn, Elsinby was invariably jolly. I paid many visits during the course of my duty, for it was a fine pub. Its drinking accommodation was one long bar with six oak beams, furnished with the inevitable dart board, yards of ale, hunting prints, sporting trophies, an open fireplace and a stone floor. It boasted a landlord for whom nothing was too much trouble and it was a foregone conclusion that his inn was very popular. An added bonus was the fact that the beer was very good. That was understandable, because it was brewed in Yorkshire.

I popped in whenever I passed through the village at lunchtime, and I popped in most evenings. I never drank on duty, but went for a chat and an opportunity to learn local gossip. At lunchtime, the locals would be swapping yarns and playing darts, and it was the same crowd that frequented the bar during the evenings. Those locals practically lived there.

Outsiders joined them for the evening sessions, but the nucleus of life in the pub was that group of local men. I was to learn, soon after my arrival that they were local farmers in the main, plus a businessman or two, a racing journalist, a doctor, the vicar, the postmaster and others of no specific occupation. Due to the nature of the people who attended so regularly, it was logical that village meetings be held in that pub. The parish council met there monthly because every councillor was in the place anyway. The British Legion committee met here too, in the shape of the same group of men, and if there was a special meeting or committee for any village function, the same people would be appointed, the meeting held and the function arranged.

In many ways it was an admirable arrangement and there was the added benefit that I knew where to find these people if they were required in a hurry, like the doctor, for example. Such an occasion arose with the death of Irresponsible John.

Irresponsible John was a tramp. He was a tall man with masses of very dark hair through which shone a scarred nose and two very dark eyes. He was like every man's idea of Fagin. His unruly mass of hair was covered by an old top hat and he wore a long, black coat with old boots and dark trousers. His hands were always gloved with a pair of very holey mits without fingers and I never saw him remove them, whether in the middle of summer or winter.

John lived in a derelict cottage on an elevated site on the edge of Elsinby, along the York road. He spent most of his time roaming the neighbourhood and earning a few shillings by casual labour, scrounging his meals from grateful farmers and smallholders. The village loved him too because he was totally harmless and honest. Everyone accepted him for what he was – a harmless old tramp of indeterminate age and unknown background. Very occasionally, he would pop into the Hopbind for a mild ale, but this was not a common practice. In the coldest spells, he would buy the occasional bottle of rum, a relic of his naval days.

I was in the Hopbind one Wednesday lunchtime when Gilbert, the postman, dashed in looking haggard and flustered. He asked for a double Scotch which was promptly handed to him and then he gasped.

"It's John, dead. At his cottage. I've just found him."

"Not Irresponsible John?" asked George, the landlord.

"Aye, John. He's up at his house."

"How did you find him?" I asked, not at that time knowing the village routine.

"Took his dinner as usual." He shrugged his shoulders and downed his drink. "Pork pie, peas and chips, done to a turn by my missus. He liked his pork pies, chips and peas, did John. I knocked, opened the door like I always do, and there he was, lying on the floor."

Doctor McGee, in his tweed plus fours, joined us. "Dead, did you say?"

"Flies all over," said Gilbert, wrinkling his nose.

"I'll go up there," I said, for I was on duty. My motor-cycle was outside, so I donned my helmet and left the pub. Doctor

Archibald McGee said he would follow in his car, and he rapidly swallowed his pint.

I knew the cottage. It was just off the York road and was a lovely place, or it had been a lovely place. It was the type of house that graces Victorian paintings, with honeysuckle around the door, roses climbing the walls, no footpath or garage, and a garden full of hollyhocks and red-hot pokers. Built of yellow limestone, it had a red pantile roof and a range of outbuildings adjoining the dwelling portion. Sadly, it was neglected and rotting, because no one admitted ownership so John had made his home there, many years ago. He demanded little of the place, save shelter from the elements. I leaned my motor-cycle against the rickety garden fence and walked somewhat apprehensively towards the front door. It was open. I inched it further against the wall and shouted, "John? Are you there?"

Wondering if Gilbert had made a mistake in his amateur diagnosis, I entered on tiptoe, feeling like a trespasser, but there in the middle of the floor of the tatty living-room was the stiff corpse of Irresponsible John. It was early autumn with a warm September day to compensate for the wet summer, and the flies were enjoying the gift nature had presented them. I have no idea how long he'd lain there, but pathologists can estimate this by the stage of development of maggots found in and upon bodies. I had no wish to determine this, nor even to examine him for their presence, but I touched the whiskery face and found it was stone cold. *Rigor mortis* had set in. That John was dead could be in no doubt.

Policemen always treat sudden and unexplained deaths with extreme caution, regarding them as murders until proved otherwise. The house did not bear signs of forcible entry, but an unlawful entry would barely have been evident here. The windows were hanging out, the doors tilted from their hinges and the place had a dark and dismal appearance inside. There was no way of knowing if anyone had broken in, but I could see no injuries upon him. It was not easy to be sure due to his mass of hair and the thick clothes in which he lay. We'd have to strip him to be absolutely sure.

A few minutes later, Dr McGee arrived, followed by the entire lunchtime population of the Hopbind Inn. As McGee

entered the house, the others remained outside, silently waiting for news. It reminded me of the crowds that used to wait
outside prisons for news of executions. McGee looked at me,
wrinkled his nose and said, "He's a bit strong, isn't he?"

"Like Gorgonzola," I heard myself comment. "He's dead,
Doctor."

McGee crouched at his side, felt the pulse, lifted the eyelids
and touched the skin.

"Dead as they come," he said. "How, I wonder?"

"You've never treated him, Doctor?" I asked.

"Once, years ago," he confirmed. "He stuck a hayfork
through his foot. Never since."

"So you can't certify the cause of his death?" I put to him
hopefully.

"Sorry," he shook his head. "I can certify that he *is* dead, so
you can set the ball rolling. But I can't certify the *cause* of
death – it looks like natural causes, I must say. There's no
indication of poisoning, no obvious marks of violence, no
sleeping tablets lying around. I think he's just faded away, Mr
Rhea, but I cannot certify that."

I groaned inwardly. This meant a post-mortem and I must
set about the task of arranging it. I would have to make
enquiries about his past and then complete reports. There
would be relatives to trace, the funeral to arrange with a
hundred other chores, to say nothing of stripping that smelly
corpse to the bare skin in readiness for the pathologist's knife.
John's remains would have to be removed as soon as possible
and taken to the mortuary at Ashfordly, the nearest place
which boasted one.

Having delivered his glad tidings, Dr McGee went outside
and told the assembly that Gilbert's diagnosis had been
correct. Irresponsible John was dead. Upon receipt of that
news, they all adjourned to the pub to drink to his memory. I
was left holding the body.

I radioed Control and asked for a message to be passed to
Sergeant Bairstow, who was the duty sergeant that day. I
asked that the van be sent from Eltering to John's cottage,
complete with the shell. The shell was a fibre-glass box,
shaped like a coffin, into which a corpse was placed for
transportation, especially for a trip to the mortuary. Sergeant

Bairstow was out, and no one was at the office. I knew he'd be at lunch, and he never answered the telephone during his refreshment break. I asked Control to try at two o'clock.

That meant I had to wait around and I didn't relish the idea of standing like a sentinel at John's gate until help arrived. I went back into the house, made a careful search for signs of violence upon him, weapons, forcible entry and all the other routine matters appertaining to a sudden death. Then I left. John wouldn't go away, so I adjourned to the pub where I broke my rule about drinking on duty. I ordered a sandwich and accepted a pint from the doctor. Like the others, I raised my glass and said, "Here's to Irresponsible John. May he roam the heavens as he did the English countryside."

By two o'clock the regulars of the Hopbind Inn had done their best to speed him to eternal happiness, and I returned to the scene to await the shell. It arrived about half past two in a police van driven by P.C. Alwyn Foxton of Ashfordly. We carried it into the house, placed it at the side of the corpse and, holding our breath, lifted John and his entourage of buzzing flies into the shell. We rammed on the lid after forcing down a stubborn arm which insisted on rising like a flagpole from his side. Then we lashed the lid with ropes in case that arm lifted it off. A rising coffin lid, with an arm that looked like someone attempting to escape, could have caused embarrassment in town. We lifted the shell by its rope handles and lugged it into the rear of the van, sliding it along the floor. No one would know we had a body in there, except the cloud of hovering flies.

We transported him to the mortuary where I formally identified him as a tramp known to me as Irresponsible John. My search of his house had revealed nothing to indicate his true name and our records would show him merely as John. With Alwyn's help, we stripped the body, searched it thoroughly for signs of injury and listed all his clothing, together with odds and ends from his pockets. We placed everything inside a locker and recorded that we found no sign of injury upon the body. John now lay starkers upon the slab.

I arranged the post-mortem for next day at Scarborough Hospital and we took him in the van, once more using the shell. The pathologist, a hawk-like fellow with staring eyes and a weird sense of humour, performed the necessary operation and pronounced that John had died from natural causes. His heart had given up its long, hard battle and he estimated that John was about eighty years old. For a man of that age, he was remarkably well preserved and surprisingly fit. He'd had a good innings.

A natural death meant there would be no inquest, which in turn meant that his funeral could go ahead. I reported this to the committee in the Hopbind Inn the following lunchtime and realised the burial was causing problems. John had no known relatives, so who was going to organise and pay for the funeral? By chance or by good fortune, the local carpenter-cum-undertaker was in the pub. He assured us he could make a coffin and carry out the funeral. The vicar said he would bury John in his churchyard, even though it was not known to which religion John had adhered throughout his wandering life. But who would pay? The assembled drinkers decided that John had been too much of a friend to the village to suffer the indignity of a pauper's grave.

It was Gilbert Kingston, the postman, who made a suggestion. He said the entire village should pay. The inhabitants numbered about four hundred and if they all paid ten shillings each towards a funeral kitty, we could send off John in a decent manner. Harold, the undertaker, reckoned that sort of money would pay for a high quality coffin with chrome handles and silver angels, a marble headstone, flowers and funeral tea afterwards. The idea seemed feasible, so it was proposed that a committee be established to make the arrangements for the interment of Irresponsible John. There was no time to lose.

I was not elected to the committee because I was not a resident of Elsinby, although it was stated that I could be co-opted if the need arose. I agreed to this. Harold would set about making the coffin and the vicar would begin the funeral arrangements. It was decided that the funeral should be at 3.30 pm the following Tuesday, at Elsinby Parish Church.

Faced with the impossible task of tracing his relatives, I told the Press who gave space to my problem in the hope that someone would claim him. I assured the committee that John could lie in state at Ashfordly Mortuary until the day of the funeral. There was nowhere else for him; besides, the mortuary was an ideal resting place and some schoolchildren picked flowers to display on the window ledge above his head.

The whole idea of a village fund was a fine one, but even before that lunchtime session was over, the racing journalist came up with a better suggestion.

"Look," he said, swilling his brandy around the glass. "If you ask ten bob from everyone in the village, you're bound to come across those who are unwilling. There'll be those who are skint, and those who are too mean. There'll be some who reckon it's not the correct thing to do. Then there's all the bother of collecting it. Why don't we raise the cash in an enjoyable way? Why not arrange a dance or something? Some kind of social event? We hold dances from time to time to raise cash for the old folks' Christmas treat, or for the church repair fund. We always get a good turn-out because folks enjoy it, so I'm sure they'd turn out for John. We could lay on a supper, and I know George would see we got a bar."

"I would that!" enthused George.

"Lots of folks would come and we'd raise a few hundred pounds. There is that lad in the council houses and his mates, who play guitars. They'd make music for us, I'm sure."

"Is the parish hall free on Saturday, Vicar?" asked Gilbert.

"It's free today and Saturday," he said. "Does that give us time to get things fixed?"

"Sure! We can run a dance. Charge ten bob per person for entry, run a bar and a raffle, lay on a supper and we'll make enough to give John a decent burial. Great idea!" George was delighted with the scheme.

And so the function was organised. I have never seen a village committee work so quickly. I left because I had to see a man about a witness statement relating to a traffic accident in York, but the committee remained on the pub premises to work upon the idea. Before tea-time that Friday evening, posters had been handwritten and distributed, the lads seen about the music, the bar arranged, the vicar had checked the heating of the hall, and the W.I. agreed to provide the supper. Their terms were half the proceeds for themselves and the other half to be allocated to the I.J.F. – the Irresponsible John Fund.

And so the great dance was fixed. It would take place in the village hall, Elsinby on Saturday night, commencing at 8.30 pm. Tickets would be ten shillings each, with supper 5 shillings extra, payable on receipt. George, the landlord of the Hopbind Inn, agreed to let all his profits, less expenses, be allocated to the Fund. The cost of hiring the hall would be waived, and so a good "do" was assured. One village elder suggested that John should lie in state during the dance, with his clean body, probably with a shave and a haircut, on display in his excellent coffin. The notion was not considered viable because he wasn't president of anything, or an archbishop.

At eight o'clock that Saturday, I presented myself in full uniform at the dance hall and was staggered by the size of the crowd. With half an hour to go, a queue was forming. The waiting people were of all types and ages – pensioners, farmers, young folk, professional people and even a smattering of visitors who had come to pay their last respects to a lovable person. The three lads who formed the group called themselves Hot Potato and were on stage, fixing their electronics and amplifiers, and tuning their guitars. They fancied themselves as the Beatles, and although their music was amateurish and noisy, with a lot of wrong notes, it was ideal for this night.

In one of the ante-rooms, the ladies of the Women's Institute were frantically laying out plates of food, each plate bearing two quarters of a sandwich, one bun and one biscuit, with an unspecified number of cups of tea being allowed per person. They had arranged a raffle, with rapidly gathered prizes like fruit cakes, bottles of spirit, a chicken or two, and several prizes of a dozen eggs.

George had installed his bar in another ante-room and although all his produce was bottled, he was guaranteed a good trade. Drinkers of draught beer would come tonight – he had ensured that by the simple expedient of closing his pub in John's honour.

The dance began with the opening tune of "Johnny was a Warrior" and the excited crowd squeezed onto the floor. The place was heaving with room only to shuffle around but everyone seemed very happy. These rural dances seldom caused any policing problems because they attracted a good quality of person, youngsters who knew how to behave in public and who respected the property and rights of others. I had managed to park all the cars around the minor roads of the village and some had squeezed onto the car park before the hall. Sergeant Bairstow arrived about ten o'clock, just to make sure things were running smoothly and he remarked upon the good nature of the dancers and the lack of fights and other trouble. He had spent a large slice of his time in one of the local towns on the borders of Middlesbrough, where trouble went hand-in-hand with Saturday night.

Out here, it was different. We had pleasant ways of enjoying ourselves. I wandered around the exterior of the hall, showing my uniform prominently as I was expected to do, and occasionally I popped in just to check that the bar wasn't full of children and that no drunkenness would spoil the evening. My worries were superfluous. The committee had everything under control.

Myself and Sergeant Bairstow purchased our suppers when the group broke for theirs, and by quarter to midnight, the dance was over. The revellers made their contented way home and I spent another hour in the village, checking that no one had broken any of the minor laws that the Government had inflicted upon us. I turned in, very happy.

When I called at the Hopbind the following lunchtime, Sunday, the committee members were earnestly counting cash. The bar was high with coins and notes, and there were little boxes marked 'raffle', 'door', 'bar' and 'supper'. A representative of the W.I. was there in the form of the husband of one of the members, and when all was totalled up, the profit was just over £800. In precise terms, it was £806 15s. 7d. George had taken out his expenses for the purchase of beer and spirits, which he allowed the committee to have at cost, while the W.I. stuck to their guns by claiming half-crowns for every supper sold. The £806 was profit after all expenses had been deducted.

Harold the undertaker reckoned that his costs would be little over £200, added to which would be the church expenses

and other incidentals, coming to around £50 at the most.
Another item of expenditure was the funeral tea. It was
customary in these moorland villages to have a funeral tea,
and it was fashionable among the best people, to have ham.
As one old lady said, "I've buried four husbands, and all with
ham."

Some twenty years before this particular burial, the funeral
would have been a long, drawn-out affair with everyone
dressed in black, and a *cortège* drawn by a black horse.
Bidders would go around the village, 'bidding' folk to attend,
and another custom was that every one attending the funeral
would pay a proportion of the cost. It was a relic of such a
custom that helped bury John in a decent grave, although the
method of raising the cash was a little at variance with past
ideals.

The committee therefore decided to organise a funeral tea
in the village hall and the W.I. accepted responsibility for
that task. The costs would come from the fund already on
hand. This was agreed. As the funeral was the following
Tuesday afternoon, I made sure the body was released on
Monday, in time to be laid in the coffin so lovingly prepared
by Harold. On the Monday evening, it was taken into the
church where it rested overnight on a bier before the altar.

By 3.30 pm on Tuesday, the church was full with mourners spilling into the churchyard as the bells tolled mournfully.
Many were dressed in the traditional black, wearing clothes
that had attended every funeral in this village for the past
century or so. The committee had found six volunteers to act
as bearers and John's grave had been dug in a peaceful
corner. As the sexton told me afterwards, "Ah laid him in
t'quietest spot, thoo knaws. Ah thowt that if he was gahin ti
pong as mich in deeath as he did in life, we'd better put him
somewhere oot of t'rooad. Ah disn't want my graveyard
smelling' o' tramps."

With the body already in church, the vicar began his
service as only Anglican vicars can. His sombre intonations
echoed around the church and sounds of sobbing could be
heard here and there, with elderly ladies sniffing into black-
edged handkerchiefs. The Reverend droned on and on, using
the formal service and then he delivered his tribute to the

dead John. He spoke in glowing terms of John's love of peace and solitude, of his godliness, of his desire never to inflict himself upon anyone and never to be a burden on society. He talked in emotional terms, but failed to remind the congregation of the time he'd asked John to leave a communion service because of the old wayfarer's pungency on a hot summer day.

He then quoted a little from Milton by reading "A death-like sleep, a gentle wafting to immortal life" and ended with Byron's words,

> "How sweet this very hour to die!
> To soar from earth and find all fears
> Lost in thy light – eternity!"

Finally, the bearers lifted the superb coffin from its wheeled-bier and carried it from the church. Everyone tried to follow it into the churchyard where the interment occurred amid more sobbing. Solemn prayers filled the air, a handful of earth was thrown into the grave to rattle on the coffin lid, and it was all over. The sexton, who was able to dig any grave in any ground and achieve straight sides, began the long job of topping it up. Everyone else made a rush for the village hall where tea, with ham, was laid on. John had been finally laid to rest. His tombstone, suitably inscribed, stood in the blacksmith's shop awaiting erection at the head of the grave.

The blacksmith was something of a stonemason too, and he had carved an epitaph upon it. It read, "John, a friend of the village", followed by the date and a small piece of prose which read, "A tombstone can neither contain his character, nor is marble necessary to transmit it to posterity". The obscurity of this phrase made it very acceptable, because no one really understood it.

The tea was a mountainous affair and it seemed that the ladies of the W.I. had talked to their grannies and elderly relations, because it was reminiscent of a funeral tea of the last century. There was ham in abundance. It was a memorable day to say the least and it lasted from the beginning of the funeral until about eight-thirty at night, with the final moments of the tea providing beer for everybody who requested it and tea for the teetotallers. When the meal was over, the drinkers adjourned to the Hopbind for further opportunities to say farewell to Irresponsible John. I went home.

I thought that would have been the end of my involvement with John, save for the occasional burst of energy in attempting to trace his relatives, but this was not the case. About a week later, I dropped into the Hopbind Inn at lunchtime and found the committee still hard at work. They welcomed me and offered to buy me a drink, but I declined because I was in uniform. A drink was therefore set aside for me next time I called off duty. It was a small 'thank-you' for my help with the funeral.

"We've all this spare money, Mr Rhea," Dr McGee told me. "Our total income from the dance was in excess of £800 as you know. The funeral costs came to £243. That left us with a balance of £563 to be precise. We laid on that funeral tea – and a right good 'do' it turned out to be. All that ham! That cost us £120, leaving us with £443, which we have placed in a deposit account with Barclays Bank. Now several folk at the tea reckoned that John's Fund should not have paid for it – they were old-fashioned folks who believed that bidden mourners should pay towards the expense. So somebody started putting money in a jug. Others followed suit and we collected £74 at the tea! That makes a balance of about £517, give or take a bob or two. We're meeting now to discus what to do with it. Damn it all, we didn't intend this. We just wanted to give John a decent funeral. So how can we spend it?"

"Have you considered a playing field for the village?" I suggested. "You've no cricket field of your own, have you? I've often talked to the youngsters of Elsinby and I know they'd love a field where they could play football and cricket."

"Now that's a grand idea," beamed George the landlord. "Aye, that's a right good idea. Jim Friend has a field, hasn't he? You remember, he tried to get planning permission to build a couple of bungalows, but they wouldn't let him. Summat to do with ribbon development, I think. It's no good for grazing because it's too sour. He might sell it, eh?"

It was therefore decided that Dr McGee, as chairman of the

committee, should approach Farmer Friend with a view to buying the field. It was reckoned there was enough land to provide space for a pitch and changing rooms/pavilions. And there was sufficient cash for all that. As they deliberated the possibilities, I felt elated. John had done a lot for Elsinby.

I called in a week later, off duty and in civilian clothes, and Dr McGee was in the bar, as usual. I got my free pint this time.

"Ah, Mr Rhea. Just the fellow. We got that field."

"That's great news!" I was delighted. "When do we start making it fit for play?"

"We've started," he told me. "But old man Friend insisted we did not pay for it. He's made his money, and he felt it was a good donation for the village. We can't get rid of John's money, can we? Anywa,, we now have a sports field, and we are busy looking at suitable pavilions."

The plans went ahead. The local reporter heard about it and did a feature in the Ryedale Weekly. The formal opening of the field, with an inaugural if late cricket match, took place one September evening and a good crowd attended. Elsinby beat Aidensfield by three runs, a good result. A small charge was made to fund the newly formed Elsinby Cricket Club, and so that project was nicely under way.

As a result, the story of Irresponsible John's benefit to the village made headlines in some of the national papers. A local T.V. station made a short feature film about the village community and in all, Elsinby hit the headlines for a brief period. The field was named after John, and is now called John's Field.

The fund continued to grow in spite of efforts to spend it, and after everything had been paid for, there was still £400 left. And it was gaining interest all the time. The fact that our story had appeared in some of the national papers resulted in the inevitable.

People began to claim relationship to John. Some said the money was theirs by right, but none of the claims could be substantiated. The committee made use of a solicitor who had a cottage in Elsinby and he reckoned the cash did not belong to any estate of John's. It belonged to the villagers, for it had been contributed by them to a fund for use by the village, and not by John. The living John had never exercised control over it. We successfully resisted every claim.

The finale came late one evening as I was patrolling Elsinby. I decided to pop into John's old house. I often did this just to check that no more dead bodies lurked there. On this night I found three living bodies – three more tramps. They had a small paraffin stove in the middle of the living-room floor and were brewing soup of doubtful origins. It was evident they intended staying.

I checked their names with our Control Room but none was wanted for any crime or for service of summonses, so I allowed them to remain. Ownership of the house was in doubt; no one seemed able to say to whom it rightly belonged and I knew that if John had been alive, he'd have welcomed his brothers of the highway. I had no power to remove them and besides, if I let them stay there, I knew where they were and what they were doing.

"We've heard about this village," one of them smiled through toothless gums. "They like tramps here, eh? They look after them, so we've come to stay."

Before Christmas, two more turned up and soon there was a colony of them in John's old house. Looking at the state of them, I felt we'd soon need some of John's Fund to bury them! I reckon he would approve of that.

Eight

Having been recruited into a predominantly rural police force, it was understandable that I should be indoctrinated with the law, practice and procedure relating to animals. Like all other bobbies, I had a lot to do with dogs, but there is a whole range of other animals which are likely to cross the path of a patrolling constable.

Because of the infinite range of possibilities stretching across thirty years of a policeman's service, our training school days were heavy with lectures and practical displays on how to cope. We were told about epizootic lymphamgitis, cattle plague, pleuro-pneumonia, foot and mouth disease and anthrax, with sundry horrors like fowl pest and rabies thrown in. We were taught about cruelty to animals and provided with detailed explanations about *cruelly* beating, over-riding, over-driving, ill-treating, over-loading, torturing or terrifying any animal. How one could perform these deeds without 'cruelly' doing them, was beyond me. There were lectures on illegal operations on animals, about performing animals, about horses, stallions, knackers' yards, birds and pet shops. We got the lot.

It would be fair to say that the lectures covered most of the problems involving animals which we were likely to en-counter during an average tour of duty in an average English county. Unfortunately, I was not given advice about coping with zebras, camels, elephants and wallabies, nor did we receive instruction about the problems of pregnant badgers and hedgehogs with their heads fast in treacle tins.

The basic training was sound, however, and one of its more enjoyable aspects was the practical demonstration. Such demonstrations were given by our instructors and one dealt with the subject of "Animals Dead or Injured in the Street".

For this, the instructional staff staged a traffic accident where a motor vehicle had knocked down and killed a domestic animal. A volunteer student had to deal with the situation from the traffic accident viewpoint and then deal with the dead or injured animal. We were told that a reportable road accident involved D. G. CHAMPS – dogs, goats, cattle, horses, asses, mules, pigs and sheep. Incidents involving other animals were not classified as "accidents" for road traffic purposes. Nonetheless, if a car ran into something pretty large like a stag or a fox, there would be work for a police officer, if only to clear the scene, to attend to any injured person or beast and to find a garage to tow off the damaged vehicle. In our dealings with animal accidents, we could be relied upon to provide nice business for the local knackers' yards.

In one of our staged incidents at training school, a pig had been run over by a car. It was dead. A pretty young police-woman was volunteered to be the "officer at the scene". She strode confidently towards the location as we stood around in a watchful semi-circle, with our pocket books open. We were to take notes too, as if we were also dealing with the matter. The procedure at a genuine accident is fairly routine and straightforward. The police take all the known details of the driver, including his name, age, occupation and address. They note particulars of the vehicle, such as its make, model, type, registration mark, details of tax and insurance, and any other factual matters which are relevant. Because the traffic flow must not be interrupted longer than necessary, the vehicle must be removed, although the animal victim must not be forgotten. If it is alive and injured, with no known owner around, a police officer can call in a vet to have it examined and, if necessary, destroyed. The expense lies at the door of the owner if and when he is found. If the vet thinks the animal can be removed without cruelty, the owner must remove it; if he refuses or is not there, the police can cause it to be removed and the owner is responsible for the bill.

It was with these considerations that our practical demonstration got under way. The instructional staff kept a large, pink model of a pig for this purpose and it lay in the road, mortally injured by a motor-car driven by a huge man, another volunteer student. This was the scene, therefore, as our little lady policeman called Susie, waded in to cope. She managed very well with the irate motorist, who blamed the pig for all his misfortunes. She calmed his shattered nerves, then took all his particulars, including measurements of the road and the position of the car. The owner of the pig was not known, nor was its place of origin revealed. She rang a vet who said he would come along to examine it and in due course, another instructor arrived, suitably clad in a white overall and plus fours. In the traditional Scots accent of a vet, he declared the pig dead.

"Now, W.P.C. Shaw," beamed the instructor, "you've made a good job of this. The pig is dead, so we are not worried about having to destroy it in a humane manner. What are you going to do with the carcase?"

"I'll have it dragged away by the knackers," she said, with all innocence.

Armed with training of that quality, I sallied forth into the vast empty spaces of the North Riding of Yorkshire. In the years prior to my posting to Aidensfield, I had dealt with one or two traffic accidents involving animals, usually dogs or cows, and these had caused no problems. Soon after my arrival at Aidensfield, however, a very harassed motorist knocked at my door late one night. I was on duty as it happened, working a late shift from 5 pm until 1 am, and was fortuitously in the house having my statutory three-quarters of an hour refreshment break. I was on my final cup of tea when the knock jerked my thoughts from the television, so I answered the door. A white-faced man stood there, leaning heavily against the door jamb. He was middle-aged with greying hair and I noticed his smart, polished shoes. He was breathing heavily and looked like a town gentleman. I could see he was perspiring slightly and wondered if he was ill.

"Good evening," I said, not being able to conjure up anything more sparkling.

"Ah!" the relief was evident in his voice. "You are a policeman?"

"Yes," I was in shirt sleeves, and he managed a thin smile when I confirmed my role.

"I've got to report an accident." He shook visibly as he spoke those words.

"Oh, come in," I stepped back and invited him into the house. "Can you manage a cup of tea?"

"Love one," he breathed, sitting heavily on a chair in the office. "Yes, I'd love one if it's no bother."

"There's one in the pot," I told him. I left him for a moment as I asked Mary to produce a cup for him, and I'd have another myself as I talked with him. I returned and found him smoking a cigarette, somewhat relieved.

"Now," I said, handing him the tea. "Accident? Was it a bad one?"

"The front of the car's all bashed in," he said. "One headlight's gone, mudguard dented, bonnet twisted slightly. This is the first police house I've found . . . "

"What did you hit?" I asked.

"A kangaroo," he said, looking at me and staring into my eyes, daring me to disbelieve him.

"A kangaroo?" My thoughts turned immediately to D. G. CHAMPS. Kangaroo was not one of the listed animals, so this was not a road accident. This meant I did not have to compile an accident report.

"It's not listed in the road traffic acts," I aired my knowledge. "You don't have to report it – accidents involving kangaroos are not reportable."

"But I hit one, officer, just down the road!"

"Are you sure it was a kangaroo?" I asked. "You are deep in the countryside, you know, and we have all kinds of animals here. Deer, badgers, foxes, hares . . . "

I'd once seen a camel striding purposefully across the moors in a heavy mist, but daren't mention that to him. It had astounded some drivers at the time, but had been hired from a local zoo by a party of schoolboys who rode it during a stunt. As I talked to him, I realised that a camel wasn't D. G. CHAMPS either, unless it qualified as 'cattle'.

"It was a bloody kangaroo," he almost shouted. "I saw it. It hopped right out of the hedge and I ran slap-bang into it. I don't know where it went – it just seemed to get knocked away and I couldn't find it."

"It's not dead, then?" I asked.

"I stopped and had a look," he said. "There was a spot of blood on the road, and on my car. But it's not around, I'm sure."

I wondered if our local vet would come to declare a kangaroo dead? Or would it have to be dragged away by the knackers? I went out to examine his vehicle and found it severely damaged, with splashes of blood here and there. I took his personal particulars and a precise location of the happening. He left me half an hour later, a little more composed. I could not put this one through the books as an accident having regard to D. G. CHAMPS. It was simply not a reportable road traffic accident. I would record it merely as an 'incident'.

But I puzzled over his kangaroo. When I resumed patrol, I decided to visit the location of his confrontation and in the headlight of my motor-cycle, found the spots of blood on the road. He'd told me of the direction from which it had leapt at him and I decided to have a look around. I guessed it had gone into the field opposite, so armed with my sturdy police torch, I parked the bike and climbed the gate, to wander across the grassy area beyond. And I found his kangaroo. It was dead, with its head badly injured. It had managed to leap this far before collapsing. But it wasn't a kangaroo. It was a wallaby, and wallabies are not part of D. G. CHAMPS either! I left it in the field, just as I would have done had it been a hare, a rabbit or other wild animal. Besides, it would be found by the farmer next morning, and it would provide a talking point in the pub for many an hour. They'd all wonder how it had arrived, and I would not tell them. It would be interesting to hear the speculation.

Next morning, I rang the motorist at his home near Middlesbrough to explain he'd been wrong. I told him it wasn't a kangaroo, but a wallaby. He laughed.

"Go on," he said. "Put me out of my misery. How can I run down a wallaby in the North Riding countryside?"

"They have some at a local zoo," I told him, "and several have escaped over the years. They've adapted to the countryside and some of them are breeding in the district. You hit a wild wallaby."

"And do you think my insurance company will swallow that?" he asked.

"Ask them to write to us," I advised him. "We'll confirm it."

That was my first brush with animals from the local zoo. Housed on a large country estate in the North Riding, the zoo was the home of a fascinating variety of animals, ranging from domestic poultry to lions and hippos, including crocodiles, flamingoes and dolphins. From time to time, some of the species did escape, although the officials were marvellous at arranging their re-capture. Because of this, exotic birds lived in the woodlands about me, and many a British ornithologist has been dumbfounded by the multi-coloured parrots, budgies and humming birds which somehow managed to survive in the bleak hills of the region, if only for the summer months. After all, it's not often you find vulturine guineafowl, scaled quail or variegated wrens in English orchards.

My next link with the zoo came as the circus arrived in town. It was a small touring circus which was scheduled to stage a series of performances within the grounds of the zoo. Many of its larger animals were to be transported by rail and this was part of a publicity stunt. The elephants would be walked from Eltering Railway Station, when they would lead a procession of other animals and acts. Some would be walked, like the monkeys and chimps, while the dangerous ones would be in cages and carried on the rear of their own transporters. They would be waiting at the railway station.

It was Sergeant Bairstow, with the usual twinkle in his eye, who called me into his office one morning.

"Ah, Nicholas," he beamed. "A nice day?"

"Very nice, Sergeant," I agreed, little knowing what he had in store for me.

"I've a nice little job for you this afternoon," he smiled. "You're to be on motor-cycle escort duty."

"Something important?" I asked.

"Yes, very," and he explained about the arrival of the circus. "You're to be at Eltering Railway Station at 2 pm. The train will arrive shortly afterwards, and when all the animals have been transferred from the train, you will lead the procession through the town. Take it along the main road and into the grounds of the zoo. It's about four miles, so it could take an hour. O.K.?"

I did not know whether to be amused or not. I'd never escorted a circus. I knew there'd be clowns, jugglers, monkeys, balloons and a host of ancillary publicity gimmicks. And I'd be escorting that lot! But orders were orders. Mounted on my trusty Francis Barnett with its aerial waving behind, I reported at the railway station. The place was alive with people, especially children, and already the waiting animals were being arranged in some sort of order. Whips were cracking, trainers were shouting, animals were calling, the music was playing . . .

"The elephant's going to lead the procession," said Sergeant Bairstow who had arrived by car. "It'll dictate the pace for the others. You ride your bike ahead of the procession – clear the route of sightseers, make a way through, prevent accidents, warn motorists of the oncoming procession. I'll be at the rear – if you meet trouble, radio for assistance."

"Yes, Sergeant."

And so I waited for the moment to begin my leadership of this curious procession. After a lot of shouting, fuss, general noise and re-arranging of vehicles and cages, the circus was ready to move. I was parked in the street, waiting for the signal to start. When I saw the column of marchers heading for me, led by a huge, grey elephant, I kicked the bike into life, waited until they were closer, and set off.

I knew elephants could walk with considerable speed and this one would dictate the pace of the entire march. Driving ahead, I soon found I had difficulty maintaining a balance upon my machine. This would be due to the very slow speed, but by travelling at a steady four or five miles an hour, I managed to keep it upright. Regular checks in the mirror on the handlebars told me the entourage was keeping pace, and I could see the bulk of the elephant immediately behind me, moving with surprising speed. I daren't look around in case I wobbled and lost my balance, and therefore relied on the mirror.

We passed several knots of people *en route;* entire villages turned out to see us pass, and motorists halted to let us through. As we approached each gathering of people, cheers rose high in the air and I felt quite proud. Then the bike wobbled again; in recent minutes, I had become aware of its liability to wobble more than it should. Perhaps my back tyre was flat? I tried to look down, but this caused me to wobble alarmingly, so I frowned and kept going, hoping that I was not going to have trouble. Finally, when I reached a long, fairly flat and straight piece of road, I ventured a careful glance behind.

The leading elephant was clutching my wireless aerial!

It had seized the slender, tough aerial with its trunk and was trotting behind, hard on my tail. Three more elephants were behind that one, all gripping the tail of the one in front, and I was leading the motley procession towards the zoo. I never lived it down. One newspaper printed a photograph of me and my elephant and captioned it, "Elephant Old Bill", while another headlined the item, "Lead Kindly Bike".

It was all good, harmless fun and besides, I got free admission to the circus for my wife and family, for my part in the publicity. All the same, I began to wonder what Sergeant Bairstow would involve me with next!

I ought to add that the zoo in question was not on my beat. It lay within the boundaries of a neighbouring beat, but I frequently found myself patrolling the locality, due to my colleague's absence on other duties, or when he was ill or attending a course. I enjoyed those duties because they were so different. On two occasions, however, I received a fright, and both occurred during the same night.

Sergeant Bairstow (who else?) asked me to visit the grounds of the zoo late one night because there was a barbecue on the site. Intoxicating liquor was being sold and the organisers had obtained an occasional licence for the function. I had to pop along to ensure they closed their bars on time and that the revellers dispersed quietly. The fun was to end at 2 am, I was told. As I was on night duty, driving a Ford Anglia car instead of my motor-cycle, I was allocated that duty. It was suggested that I make my visit fairly late, in order that my presence would jolt the memories of the organisers.

I decided to visit the barbecue at 1.45 am. I drove into the car-park and was surprised to see it was deserted. I left the police car there, placed my peaked cap upon my head, grabbed a torch and walked towards the buildings of the zoo. There was not a sound from the place, save the twittering of birds and the grunts of sleeping animals. I reasoned that if there was a barbecue, there would be sounds of people and music; there'd be cars around the place and lights. But there was nothing.

In the stillness of that night, I stood with ears straining, listening for sounds of merry-making. But there was none. The place was deserted. Even the animals were asleep.

Because I knew the zoo's geography fairly well, I had a look around. I knew there were certain areas which were ideal for such an occasion, like open fields, a picnic area or the lawns before the mansion. I made a systematic search but found nothing. I did not even find any trace of a recent event, let alone a current one. I veered towards the big house, hoping that lights inside might indicate a celebration of some kind, but all was in darkness. From there, I searched the out-buildings, but again drew a blank. It was at this stage that I began to wonder if this was one of Sergeant Bairstow's quiet pieces of fun. To be completely sure in my own mind, I made a second tour of the entire zoo, but drew another blank. There was no barbecue here. I was sure of that.

I returned to the car because it was almost two-thirty in the morning and I was hungry. My refreshment period was overdue, and I was to take it at Eltering Police Station, where there was a kettle.

I began to re-trace my steps in the general direction of the car park and was cutting between some buildings when I became aware that someone was following me. My own feet made little or no noise because I wore brothel-creepers, boots with thick crêpe soles. But I could hear a woman's footsteps immediately behind me. The delicate clipping sound of high heels moved along with me. My hair stood on end. I stopped. So did the woman. I looked behind, and there was nothing, only total silence.

I wondered if I had imagined it all and set off again. The striking footsteps renewed themselves. Clip clop, clip clop, right behind me. I stopped and whirled around. There was nothing. By this time, a cold sweat was making my back most uncomfortable and my hair was standing sharply upright about the nape of my neck. No one had said the zoo was haunted, not even Sergeant Bairstow. And I didn't think he would lay on a ghost, especially at two o'clock in the morning. Or would he?

I walked again, rapidly this time, but the terrifying foot-steps came with me, moving in time with my strides. I knew the sound of a woman's high-heeled shoes, and this was definitely that sound. There was no doubt about it. I had my torch and after stopping a few times, I decided I must catch the woman, or the prankster. I had decided it was one of my colleagues playing a joke. There was no other explanation.

To complete my plans, I walked rapidly along the narrow path which ran between a building and a wall. The wall was shoulder height and I strode purposefully along, then sud-denly whirled around and shone my torch directly behind me. There was nothing. Not even Sergeant Bairstow.

I was almost at my wits' end to know what it was, when I heard a snuffling sound at the other side of the wall. I shone my torch over and found a zebra in its compound. I talked to it, switched off my torch and moved on. The clip-clop came with me. I stopped, shone my torch and there she was beside me. It was the zebra, moving along with me in her com-pound. Every time I stopped, so did she. I walked backwards and forwards along that wall, and all the time she repeated her trick. I wished I had some food for her, but I hadn't. I left her rather sadly, for she was infinitely more beautiful and far more interesting than the non-existent barbecue!

When I rang Sergeant Bairstow from Eltering Police Station and mentioned the missing revelry, he laughed and said, "I must have got the wrong night, Nicholas."

I didn't mention the zebra and wondered if he would bring up the matter at a later date, but he didn't. He went to bed and after my welcome breakfast, I resumed patrol at three-thirty. There were two-and-a-half hours before knocking off time. To fill in the lonely hours, I drove along the main road from Eltering and turned off beyond the Black Bull Inn. This would take me back into the general area of the zoo, albeit from another direction. I might just come across the site of the barbecue, in a field near the zoo, maybe?

As I drove along, I kept my eyes open for the bus shelter

which stands at the junction. I used that shelter as a kind of landmark, knowing that I had to make a sharp right turn at the point. As my headlights picked out the re-assuring shape of the shelter, I was surprised to see it was full of dogs. They were lying or standing in the bus shelter, and there would be six or eight in all. I couldn't be sure of the exact number. As my lights lit the interior, I realised they were Alsatians, so I pulled up directly opposite as they watched me with baleful eyes. Two of them came to the front of the car and sniffed at the engine, then peered into the headlamps, which I had switched off to leave only side lights.

As the engine ticked over, I racked my brains. Who bred Alsatians around here? I thought of sheep worrying and the chaos they could cause if they became savage. Clearly, some-one's breeding kennels had been left open, allowing the animals to wander off as a pack.

A pack?

My hair stood on end. For the second time that night, I was terrified. One of those 'dogs' came to my window and peered up at me. I saw that its eyes were yellow and that it wasn't an Alsatian. There was some white about it, its tail was longer, the slope of its legs was different, the coat was thicker – and those yellow eyes . . . !

Wolves. This was a pack of wolves! I recognised them now. It was a pack of Canadian timber wolves and I knew where they'd come from. The zoo. I was horrified when I realised what might have happened if they'd taken a walk near that zebra, with me as an object of pursuit. It didn't bear thinking about.

Feeling as if I was in a safari park, I sat in the safety of the car as they sniffed around it before returning to their shelter. They seemed content to remain there but I was in a quand-ary. If I left them to seek aid, they could wander anywhere and might harm cattle or sheep. If I remained here, how could I inform the zoo? My thinking must have been rather slow, probably due to the hour, for I remembered the car had a radio. I called up Force Control Room and asked them to contact the zoo, even though it was about four o'clock in the morning. The message was that their Canadian timber wolves were in a bus shelter just south of Eltering.

Within forty-five minutes, there arrived a van containing three men armed with two big nets. With remarkable dexterity, they coaxed the docile animals into the van, where they seemed like pets, and not in the least savage. It transpired they were not dangerous to humans, but I wouldn't have given them the chance. It seemed that someone had slipped open the door of their compound, but we never traced that person.

I clambered into my warm bed just after six that morning, and Mary muttered, "Had a busy night?"

"I've been trapping Canadian timber wolves," I said with as much nonchalance as I could muster.

"Wolves?" she murmured sleepily.

"Yes," I said, snuggling down against her warmth.

"Not polar bears?" she asked, moving away from my chilly feet and sinking into a deep sleep.

* * * *

A persistent animal problem came in the shape of Miss Fiona Lampton's pony. Miss Fiona spoke with a horsy accent, dressed in horsy clothes and mixed with horsy people. She had a horsy face with matching teeth and it could be said that even her laughter had a ring of the equine. She was a spinster of the parish, aged about thirty-eight years, give or take a little, and she lived on private means. She had no known occupation but was never short of cash; somehow she contrived to run a large, sporty car which was seldom clean, but always in a hurry.

She kept several horses but one of them was a pony, a delightful creature with a long, straggly mane and an equally straggly tail. The unfortunate animal caused me lots of problems because it had mastered the ability to open the gate of its paddock. Having perfected this trick, it would regularly unlatch the gate and take an unaccompanied stroll down the village street of Aidensfield. Horses were not unusual in our village street, but this one, whose name was Topsy, had a liking for lawns, garden flowers and lettuce. This made it rather unpopular.

During its perambulations, it would push open garden

gates or simply wander through the new open-plan estate, there to feast upon the flavour of the month, sometimes tulips, sometimes dahlias and occasionally prize chrysanthemums. Many complaints were levelled at Miss Fiona but they seemed to slide from her masculine shoulders like rainwater from a plastic mac. She agreed that Topsy was a naughty boy, in fact a bloody naughty boy at times, and she promised she would make him behave. Several villagers suggested a change of both latch and field, but she explained that Topsy was like Houdini – he could open any latch.

Eventually the problem landed on my doorstep. One or two of the more vociferous villagers decided it was time to do something official. In their eyes, that meant action by the constabulary.

I listened to their listed complaints and suggested they sent bills for damage to Miss Fiona; several had already considered that action and had sent bills, which had been promptly paid. One or two had made their garden gates more difficult to open, but as Miss Fiona said, Houdini the horse could open them. The villagers had wisely decided that a padlock on Fiona's field was not a good idea because other people required access via that field to their own premises. Locks were therefore beyond consideration. Miss Fiona had tried placing Topsy in different paddocks, but he opened those gates too. If he wandered from the nearest paddock, into the village street, at least we knew where he was.

I promised I would do what I could, but the truth was I had no idea what to do. Everything that was possible had apparently been done, both by Miss Fiona and by the villagers. The pony seemed unstoppable.

I wondered if she should be asked to sell it, then a day or two later I met the lady in the street. She cried, "What ho, Officer," and slapped her thigh with a riding crop.

"Ah!" I hailed her. "Miss Fiona. Just the person – I'd like a word with you."

"Is it about that bloody animal of mine?"

"The pony," I confirmed. "Yes, there's been a complaint, from several villagers."

"He is a bloody nuisance, Officer, and no doubt about it. A downright bloody nuisance. I can't keep him in that field, or any field for that matter. Daren't put locks on, what? Might cause problems of rights of way and things. Damned nuisance, isn't he?"

"You've horses in that top field of yours," I reminded her. "Couldn't Topsy go in there? He might like the company of other horses, and that might encourage him to stay."

"Not on your bloody nerve, Officer," she cried, horrified. "I keep my best animals in there – they'd kick poor old Topsy to death. No, I can't do that."

"He's a danger to traffic," I said. "There could be an accident."

"Not with Topsy, Officer, not with Topsy," she boomed. "Marvellous on the road, you know, better than a dog even. Hears oncoming cars and gets in the side. No problems there."

"He eats people's flowers and growing vegetables. One chap reckons he lost an entire garden full of prize dahlias."

"I paid, I always do. Good compensation. They'll have to tolerate Topsy, Officer. There's nothing I can do, I'm sorry."

"You could sell him."

"Sell him? He was a gift from an admirer of mine! No, I couldn't sell him, he's a real pet."

"Miss Fiona," I said, trying to appear threatening. "I might have to consider a prosecution, for letting him stray on the highway."

"If you must, you must," she said, and stalked away, thrashing her thigh with the crop. I watched her stride down the street, her body swaying in time with her leg movements, and I wondered what the answer could be. I didn't want to book the woman, but if she persisted in allowing Topsy the freedom of the main street, it would be necessary. It would be necessary too, if I was to appease the villagers; at least it would prove I had done *something*. If Sergeant Blaketon heard about it, he'd start asking questions and he'd demand a prosecution. But would court action stop the horse?

It was perhaps fortunate that Sergeant Bairstow met me a few days later and asked if I had any problems. I thought it a fine opportunity to discuss the pony, as he was such a seasoned and experienced police officer.

He listened carefully with his gentle smile and when I had

concluded, he said. "I don't think we need report her for summons, Nicholas. I mean, it's a well-behaved animal, isn't it? It's not dangerous to people – it doesn't go around biting and kicking them. It knows what to do in traffic and it doesn't cause severe problems."

"It eats flowers and lettuce," I reminded him.

"That's a civil matter, lad, not a crime. And she pays compensation. What more can the injured parties expect? We must not involve ourselves with civil matters."

"I must do something, Sergeant. That woman must be taught that the pony is her responsibility."

He smiled faintly. "Suppose it wasn't a horse or a pony. Suppose you found it. What would you do?"

"I don't follow." I had to admit I was confused.

"Well, suppose it was a pet cat or a dog, or something like a hamster or little lad's rabbit. You found it in the street. What would you do?"

"I'd take it to the owner's house, if I knew where that was."

"Exactly, Nicholas," he smiled again. "And suppose the owner was out?"

"I'd put it somewhere safe until they returned."

"Of course you would," he said. "I mean, if the kitchen door was open, you'd probably pop it in there, wouldn't you? Or if a hen-house was open, you'd use that . . . "

"She has no hen-houses," I said. "And her stables are locked when the horses are in the fields."

"But she always leaves her kitchen door open, doesn't she?"

"Does she?" I asked, surprised at his local knowledge.

"Always," he nodded gently. "We had trouble with her once before – it was a randy stallion she kept. It fancied everything from articulated lorries to poodles, and I often called to see her about it. She sold it to a circus, I think. I've no idea what kinds of tricks it got up to. I seem to remember they had to keep the elephants out of its way."

"You're not suggesting I put it in her kitchen, are you?" I asked, horrified at the suggestion.

"I wouldn't suggest a thing like that, Nicholas!" he said, leaving me to my thoughts.

During that summer, I must have received a further half-dozen complaints about Miss Fiona's pony, and one day I was in the village street when Topsy came trotting along, utterly alone.

This was my moment of decision. I was faced with the problem in person.

"Topsy!" I shouted, and the pretty pony came willingly to me. It nuzzled its face under my arm and I patted its head, as it rubbed itself against me.

"You've done it again," I heard myself say to the animal. "Come along, it's time for action."

Holding its long mane, I walked the length of the street and several villagers smiled their greetings. I said I was taking Topsy home for tea, and they smiled, some with happiness and other with expressions of bewilderment. I reached her house. It was a lovely cottage with a large white gate opening onto the road. Inside the gate was a converted farmyard, with outbuildings all around, all locked. Her cottage was on the left as I entered. It had a white door of the old stable-door type, and this led directly into her kitchen.

I knocked.

There was no reply. I reached up for the latch of the top half of the door and found the pony's muzzle nudging my hand. It managed to press the sneck and the door swung open on oiled hinges, swinging with its own weight to rest inside the kitchen.

"Clever stuff," I stroked its head. "Can you smell the metal or something?"

I reached down for the lower sneck but the intelligent animal was with me. With its nose, it depressed the handle and the door swung open, to lodge beneath the upper half. The way into the kitchen was clear. I led Topsy inside and left him standing on the tiled floor, as I closed the door behind myself. I didn't think he could let himself out because the doors would only open inwards – whether the horse would reason that, I did not know. But I left the house feeling very happy. Fiona now had a horse in her kitchen. I was to learn later, that this had registered in Topsy's head. Each time he let himself out of his field, he made his unerring way to the kitchen, opened the door and let himself in.

It would be several weeks later when I met Miss Fiona.

"Ah, Officer!" she beamed. "I've good news for you."

"Really?" I wondered what it could be.

"Topsy!" she said. "He's with a riding school at Eltering now. I donated him on a permanent-loan basis. He remains my property, but they use him for lessons; they feed him and so on. Good wheeze, eh? He'd found a way of opening my kitchen doors you know. Let himself in, opened the bloody fridge and pinched all my vegetables and fruit. The bloody animal!"

"He's an amazing horse," I smiled. "Very intelligent."

"Too bloody intelligent!" she laughed.

When I told Sergeant Bairstow, he smiled quietly. "It was better than taking her to court over the pony," he said.

"Yes, it was," and I knew the villagers regarded my action as being very correct. Several asked if I had considered joining the Royal Canadian Mounted Police.

Nine

With an abbey full of Benedictine monks virtually on my doorstep, it was not unexpected that I should become involved with the church in one or more of its forms. Life within the shadows of an abbey was fascinating – the Benedictines of Maddleskirk are Roman Catholics but their philosophy is that all men are children of God and therefore to be treated with the respect due to them. There were precious few religious barriers and even members of the Wee Frees of Scotland would find a welcome within the portals of that mighty Christian church, an invitation that was not expected to be reciprocated. But true men of God are full of forgiveness.

Monks in long black cloaks, or tee-shirts and jeans, or sports gear, wandered about our countryside and were part of the scenery. Because they were a living part of the local populace, they had lost a lot of their mystique. The villagers found the monks very human, very kindly and very knowledgeable, as was expected of an ancient and historic teaching order, and it was not unusual to find oneself enjoying a pint of beer in the pub, with a monk standing next to one, also enjoying a pint.

Soon after my arrival in Aidensfield, I discovered that their local ecumenical movement had already started. The two chief faiths of the district, Anglican and Roman Catholic, were friends. They shared churches, they shared services and they even shared priests. The latter came as a surprise to me, having been schooled in the village the Reformation had missed, i.e. Egton Bridge in North Riding's lovely Eskdale. I had been reared in the ancient Roman Catholic faith which tended to isolate Catholics from other faiths, but out here, this thriving Catholic monastery was the centrepiece of rural life where other faiths were openly accepted and the views of their adherents respected.

This important lesson was given to me about nine-thirty one Sunday. It was a bleak, wintry morning with sleet in the air and a powerful easterly wind blowing across my exposed hilltop. I was enjoying a week-end free from police duties, when Sunday morning meant attending Mass with the family. We had breakfasted and were washing up in the kitchen when I spotted a bedraggled figure at my garden gate. He was propping a pedal cycle against a gate post and through my steamed-up window I watched him enter the garden and make for the front door. His head was bowed against the driving sleet and his clothes blew in the cruel wind.

I dried my hands as I went to answer the door and found a young man standing before me, sensibly dressed in heavy cycling gear. He was saturated about the face and feet, his outer clothes were dripping and he looked nigh frozen to death.

"Good morning," he smiled apologetically, the words finding difficulty in leaving his frozen face. "I wonder if I might use your telephone?"

"Certainly," I agreed, bidding him enter the house. He did, and I closed the door. It was bitterly cold outside; the temperature was dropping and it wouldn't be long before the sleet turned to snow. And with this wind, there'd be problems in this locality. Lanes would become blocked with drifts and lonely farmsteads would be cut off. But all that was later . . . now, I led him into the office where his dripping clothes would not damage anything. He stood on my polished floor, making pools on the shining surface.

"Are you going far?" I asked, surprised that anyone would cycle in this weather.

"Crampton," he rubbed his hands to encourage circulation. "At least, I was. My bike's got a puncture and I wanted to ring the abbey for help."

"The abbey?" I wondered if he was talking about a pub.

"Maddleskirk Abbey. I'm a monk," and he opened his waterproofs to reveal his dog-collar. "I'm on my way to Crampton to play the organ for the ten o'clock service."

"Oh!" that explained his journey. "I see," and I then pondered slightly. "But you're Catholic monks, aren't you? Crampton Parish Church is Church of England?"

"That's right," he smiled. "The vicar rang us up in a panic. It seems his organist fell ill last night with 'flu, and he asked if we could help. The Abbot agreed, as he always does, so I'm *en route* to play their hymns like a good Anglican."

"I thought Catholics weren't allowed to attend Protestant services?"

"They weren't. It's a long story, as you know; the differences between our faiths are historic, and the Abbot regards our churches as two sisters who aren't on speaking terms. It's a temporary state of affairs, in his opinion. Eventually, they will learn to speak with one another and then I'm sure we'll find we have a lot in common. The Reformation did a lot of harm, but in the end it will be shown to have done a lot of good. In the end, we'll all be one church again, just as God intended. This is just one of the ways our Abbot has of making those two silly sisters take a long close look at each other, and to make them realise that they do share a lot of common ground."

"He sounds a very sensible man," I said.

"He is, he'll go far. Now, could I use your phone please? I'll get the monastery garage to send a car out for me."

"I'll run you down," I offered. "It's only a couple of miles."

And so I did. I said I'd ring the Abbey upon my return and arrange collection of his cycle, as I'd be at Mass myself, in the village Catholic church. I did that and later that afternoon, I mended the puncture in his back wheel. He called a day or two later and had a cup of tea, telling me he'd welcomed the experience of playing in an Anglican church. He'd enjoyed listening to the hearty Anglican singing. It transpired that the vicar hadn't announced him as a visiting Catholic monk, but had simply identified him as a visiting priest, without telling the congregation of his faith or place of origin.

"Isn't that cheating?" I asked. "Surely those good Anglicans should have known you were a Catholic? They would think you were a visiting member of their own faith?"

"Does it matter?" he asked me. "I was there to play the organ not to convert them or to argue about religion. I think one old lady summed it up afterwards – she came to me, shook me by the hand and said, 'That was fine playing, vicar'. She said it was plain to see I was a man of God. She was right, you know."

And off he went. I saw him cycle past several times in the future and he always waved.

My next spell of duty involving the church came with a telephone call from a passing motorist.

"Ah!" he said breathlessly into the mouthpiece. "Is that the policeman?"

"It is," I confirmed.

"Oh well, there's been an accident. There's a car on its roof between Thackerston and Aidensfield. It's in a field, just past the quarry," and he rang off before I could ask for more details.

It was about ten o'clock in the morning, and he'd caught me just before I left the office on my rounds. I told Mary I was just popping down the road to deal with an accident, and there I'd be for about an hour. The Sergeant could find me there, if he came visiting.

Mounted on my trusty motor-cycle, I drove slowly down the gently sloping incline which led from my house into the village of Thackerston, about two miles away. I sought indications of the accident, but arrived in Thackerston without finding any sign of trouble. Had it been a hoax call?

The fields lay to the south of the road and I'd kept my eyes peeled as well as I could while riding a motor-cycle and watching the road ahead, but there was nothing. There were no signs on the road, no broken glass, no deposited mud, no skid marks or other debris. I began to feel sure I'd been dragged out on a false call. I mounted the bike and made the return journey, remembering that the caller had mentioned the quarry. The quarry lay roughly between the two villages, so I parked my motor-cycle near its entrance and walked along the verge, seeking the accident.

And then, as I peered over the hedge at that point, I saw a car on its roof in the field. It was half-way down a steep incline and invisible from the road. I clambered over the drystone wall and ran down the grassy slope to the vehicle, but it was empty. It was a tiny black Austin A30, the successor of the Austin 7 and ancestor of the BMC Mini. There it was, finely balanced on its roof, rocking to and fro as I touched it. There was a distinct whiff of petrol but little sign of damage, other than a dented roof. I looked for the injured people, but there wasn't a soul around. I made a note of the registration number from which I could trace the owner, and returned to the road.

Once there, I sought indications of a battle with steering or brakes, but found none. Judging by its position, it had left the road, run across the wide grass verge and dived through the hedge without even attempting to brake or change course. Its point of entry into the field had been precisely where a drystone wall and a hawthorn hedge met – the car had bolted through them at that exact place. The hedge had parted and had closed after it, thus leaving no trace of its remarkable journey. It had nose-dived into the steep field and had rolled over several times, to end its trip upside down.

I rang Durham Taxation Authority, with whom the car was registered and learned that it belonged to a vicar from that part of the world. Having not heard from anyone about this accident, other than the anonymous caller, I rang his home address and a woman answered.

"Mrs Dwyer?" I asked, hoping I was talking to the wife of the Rev. Sidney Dwyer.

"Yes?" there was a question in her voice.

"I'm P.C. Rhea of Aidensfield, in the North Riding," I began.

"Ah!" she said. "My husband said you might ring. Is it about his car?"

"Yes it is, as a matter of fact."

"Well," she said. "He was on his way to Filey with three of his colleagues, where they are attending a conference. He ran off the road, near Thackerston, he tells me, but no one was hurt. They flagged down passing cars and got lifts to the conference. They're all very well, and he rang a garage to arrange removal of his car."

"Oh," I was pleased at his efficiency. "He's got it all organised."

"He's very good at organising," she said. "I do hope there's no problems."

"No," I assured her. "No problems, so long as you know about it."

"Thank you for ringing," she sounded very pleasant. "He'll call in on the way back for you to see his insurance and licence, by the way."

"He thinks of everything," I said.

"Yes, he does, doesn't he?" and she rang off. But even now, all those years later, I marvel that a car full of people could leave a road, cross a wide grass verge and plunge through a hedge without leaving a mark of any kind. And then to land upon its roof without causing any injury to its four inmates. It was a tiny car, so perhaps they'd been so tightly packed that they'd escaped injury?

It was almost as if the hand of God had lifted the little car off its wheels and plonked it upside down in the field. But why would He want to do that?

*   *   *   *

Lairsbeck is a hamlet some miles off my beat, and it lies deep in the North Yorkshire moors, hidden in a timbered valley called Lairsdale. It comprises a scattering of farm-steads, a telephone kiosk, some ant hills, a pillar box and the chapel. The chapel is the dominant feature. It was erected in that upsurge of religious fervour that followed Wesley across these remote parts, and it stands on the road side just beyond the first clump of pines after the watersplash. The door is of oak and very strong but inside the walls are covered with flaking whitewash and the whole place smells musty and damp.

The chapel is not used very often, perhaps once a month at the most, which means that modern heating and lighting systems are luxuries the tiny congregation cannot afford. The full congregation totals eleven, and they rely on oil lamps and paraffin heaters for light and warmth.

The task of filling the heaters had long been in the hands of Joshua Atkinson while his wife, Martha, looked after the lights. Other chapel folks had jobs like dusting, sweeping, winding up the clock, storing hymn books and stocking the tiny place with flowers. Everyone had a job of some kind, which was one way of ensuring they attended services.

That ploy gave some indication of the wisdom of Pastor Smith. He was a cunning old character, I found, and I liked him. He did not live at Lairsbeck but commuted to this outpost once a month; I met him in Ashfordly from time to time. He once told me of his first days with this small congregation.

It seemed they did not want to stand as he entered the chapel to begin the service, and this was something he felt was a vital part of the proceedings, a show of respect for him and his office. He had spoken of this from the pulpit on one occasion, and asked them to stand up next time he entered. They did not obey. He repeated his request from the pulpit but the sturdy and stubborn congregation refused to get to their feet as he entered the body of the chapel. Then he realised they always stood up to sing their hymns, and he hit upon the bright idea of having an entrance hymn as he walked towards his pulpit.

Sure enough, as the organ burst into life, they all leapt to their feet and launched into their favourite hymn as Pastor Smith moved down the aisle with a smile of satisfaction upon his face. But that was the last time they stood up, even for hymns. He told me the tale, and one of his flock told me the same tale one afternoon, over tea at his farm.

"Yon's a crafty aud sod," the farmer said. "By, he thowt he'd tricked us inti standing up for him, but nivver again. He'll nivver trick us again like that – we allus sings hymns sitting doon now, just in case he's trying to catch us out again."

It would be late on autumn afternoon when Pastor Smith hailed me in Ashfordly. "I'd like a word with you," he said.

I stopped and listened.

"I try to get men and women from the professions to read a lesson in my chapel, at the Lairsbeck services," he began. "I've had doctors, shop keepers, veterinary surgeons, and many others. Would you read for me one Sunday evening, Mr Rhea?"

It was a bolt from the blue. I'd never been to a Methodist service in my life, and told him of my own faith. He seemed surprised to find a Catholic policeman, but was even more surprised when, bearing in mind the monk and the organ playing, I said, "I'll have a word with the Abbot of Maddleskirk. If he agrees, I'll read for you."

The Abbot agreed; in fact, he was very enthusiastic and one Sunday evening in late autumn, therefore, I found myself driving to Lairsbeck in my own car and off duty, but in full uniform. I was on my way to read the lesson at Pastor Smith's tiny moorland chapel. I arrived twenty minutes before we were due to start and met him in what was akin to the vestry in my own church. He showed me the relevant passages and I read them to familiarise myself with the phraseology before my moment of glory. I said I'd be fine. He thanked me and wished me luck.

"Oh," he said, almost as an afterthought. "Be sure to sit in the seat directly beneath the pulpit."

I didn't question the wisdom of this, but nodded and we later entered the church. They were singing one of their hymns, sitting down as was their practice, and I made my way self-consciously to the seat he had advised. I noticed the little church was cosy and the oil lamps flickered in the draughts of the place, giving the building a very homely atmosphere. I knew that Pastor Smith had a reputation for long sermons, and hoped he would deliver a short one tonight. I had no idea of the progression of a chapel service but waited for the nod from him. Eventually, the signal came and I entered his varnished pulpit, cleared my throat and read the relevant passages. As I returned to my seat, he mounted the stairs and began his sermon. It went on and on. I knew I was in for a long session, for his theme was "Christianity in Practice", a talk about the benefits of ecumenism.

He spoke well, I must admit, and his words made sense, but after half an hour, I could hear the restless sounds of shifting feet, of rubbed hands, of coughing. He ploughed on regardless. I was nice and cosy beside the heater, and it wasn't an unpleasant experience.

Eventually, it was all over and they drifted away, the caretaker remaining behind to lock up and put out the lamps. Pastor Smith bade them farewell until next month and invited me to his home. "I've some explaining to do. Can I tempt you to my manse at Ashfordly? For a bite of supper, perhaps and a cup of tea?"

I agreed and followed him home. His wife produced some home-made scones and cakes and we sat to enjoy a marvellous supper. His eyes twinkled as he told me the story.

"You'll know old Joshua Atkinson?" he asked.

"Oh, yes," I knew him all right. "Queer old character, isn't he?"

Joshua was a farmer in the area, a stalwart of his chapel and one of the old school whose life-style had not changed since Wesley's visit to these parts.

"Well," said Pastor Smith. "He looks after the heaters, and his wife does the lamps. On winter Sundays, when we have services, Joshua comes down to the chapel just before lunch and fills the heaters. He lights them so the church will be warm by evening. By seven on the chilliest Sunday, the place is lovely and cosy, and you can sit without a coat. But Joshua, I found, is very cunning. He's got it off to a fine art. He'll fill the heaters just long enough to last a certain time, time for one very short sermon. If I go on too long, the heaters dry up and the congregation begins to feel cold. So do I. It is Joshua's method of telling me to belt up and go home. The crafty old monkey tries to dictate the length of my sermons.

"When he got the television installed, he would put even less paraffin in! He wanted to get home to watch his favourite programme. Well, tonight, I took my own paraffin, and I filled the heaters in the pulpit and beside your seat. He'd already filled them at lunchtime, putting in enough for his purpose. But I put more in. As Joshua and his cronies sat shivering, you and I were nice and warm, Mr Rhea. I'm sorry I went on a bit, but it was done to teach them a lesson."

I laughed aloud. "You've got to be crafty to beat this lot!" I said. "It wouldn't surprise me if they realised what you were doing!"

"He doesn't know yet, but it won't take long," Pastor Smith laughed. "It's not the first time I've filled my heater to make it last a little longer, so I'm sure he'll work it out. He judges his own fillings by the little chapel clock."

"The clock?"

"Yes, on the wall. It's an old clock. He knows how much

paraffin will last per hour, and he fills the heaters accordingly."

"The crafty old blighter!"

"But I alter the clock!" chuckled Pastor Smith. "I always get here before him, in time to fix my heater and to change the pointers of the clock. That means that his timings for the consumption of paraffin are not accurate."

"What good does that do?" I asked, puzzled by the complexity of this.

"When he realises what I'm doing," smiled Pastor Smith, "He'll work out new amounts of paraffin for the heaters, and he'll base them on the clock. But the clock is always wrong, you see, so he'll never get it right, will he? I shall work things always to my advantage. Joshua will always shiver, Mr Rhea, and I shall always be warm."

I wondered where this little drama was going to end, and left the manse very amused by it all. As I drove home, I wondered what Pastor Smith would do next in his attempts to make them stand up as he entered. Perhaps he'd play the National Anthem? I decided to suggest this to him next time we spoke.

*   *   *   *

Contrary to popular belief, the monks of Maddleskirk are a worldly crowd, closely in touch with our modern society and its attendant problems. They know about the public's concern over sin and sex, money and motoring, they take part in village affairs and county matters. Some sit on councils and one became chairman of the local District Council. Others take leading roles in teaching, sport, drugs education, religion and a host of other extramural subjects. In short, they know more about life than many of our so-called progressive society.

In spite of their many external interests, they are intensely religious and their daily routine centres upon their faith. It is probably fair to say that their Catholic faith is more important then any other aspect of life, and there are times when this overlaps with my duties.

On one occasion, I was summoned via the radio on my

motor-cycle to a fire in Aidensfield. A cottage was burning, with smoke pouring through the roof and upper windows. Someone had phoned my house; I was out, engaged upon a routine patrol and Mary had the presence of mind to contact me via Control Room. I was only five minutes away and arrived at the scene to find a gaggle of onlookers staring at the smoke which was permeating through the multitude of gaps about the cottage. It rose, black and thick, through the roof, the windows and the woodwork, but no one had entered to seek its occupants.

"Is anybody in there?" I shouted as I ran to the door.

"It's old Mr Blenkinsopp," twittered one old lady. "It's his house and it's locked."

During a two-week fire fighting course a member of the R.A.F. had taught me that the opening of a door or a window could introduce fresh oxygen to the seat of a fire and that could cause it to burst into flame. At the moment, the place seemed to be gently smouldering, producing lots of smoke but no flames. Should I break down the door or not? I had to get inside somehow, and in those precious seconds of indecision, the Fire Brigade arrived.

"There might be somebody in here," I shouted.

"We'll have to break in then," returned a leading fireman. "We'll contain any blaze that erupts."

As they organised themselves, I ran to a ground-floor window and cracked it with my gloved fist, opened it and climbed in. The place was full of choking fumes and I covered my face with a handkerchief as I raced through the downstairs rooms. There was no one here. I ran upstairs and as I reached the half-way stage, the front door collapsed behind me and a fireman appeared, silhouetted in the doorway. He ran upstairs behind me. I found a bedroom with billowing smoke pouring from it, and inside I could see the still figure lying on a smouldering bed. Poor old Mr Blenkinsopp.

Coughing madly, I went to him, but it was far, far too late. His body was the colour of brown varnish, his clothing smouldered to ashes and his extremities burnt away. He had no feet or hands, no hair and his hot body was swollen with a combination of fire, gas and intense heat. I heard a loud thump behind me; the fireman had fainted at

the sight, but another rushed in with a hose and asked,
"What shall I do?"

"Switch the electricity off," I shouted at him. "It's an
electric blanket." The tell-tale cable ran from beneath the
remains of the bed, and he switched off the mains supply.

"Shall I spray the bed?"

"Please."

No. 1 fireman had recovered and together, they sprayed the
red-hot bed and the heated corpse with their small hose.
Fortunately, nothing else was burning and all that had been
destroyed was the bed. Nothing else had caught fire. Smoke
had discoloured the upper rooms and some places downstairs;
even the windows bore a covering of slimy brown fumes, but
happily, the close atmosphere had prevented the flames breaking out. We later discovered that the bed had smouldered
literally all through the night, and that poor old Mr
Blenkinsopp took drugs. He was also an alcoholic. The post-
mortem later revealed he had gone to bed heavily laced with
barbiturates and whisky, and had left his blanket switched
on. He'd probably wet himself while asleep, an action which
could cause an electrical short in the blanket, and that in turn
could cause the smouldering. He'd died by inhaling the fumes
of the burning mattress, and would have been dead long
before the heat began to consume his body. He would have
felt no pain.

The firemen extinguished the burning bed and doused the
entire room with water, for it was hot all over. Even the
wooden beams and floor were hot to the touch and the
curtains might have blazed, the rugs too, or the bedding
which had slipped to the floor. Miraculously, nothing had
burst into flames, the house was intact and no other damage
had been done. When the firemen left, I had to remain with
the body until I could arrange its removal, and as I waited in
the room, taking the necessary notes for my report, I was
aware of footsteps on the landing. A monk appeared in the
doorway. He did not faint, but smiled and made the sign of
the cross.

"Hello, Father," I said, wondering why he had come.

"Oh," he said, "I'm pleased it's you, Nicholas. Join me in
prayer, would you? He was one of our flock, although he

never came to church in his later years. I'd like to pray at his side for a few moments."

And so I found myself kneeling before the charred remains of this unfortunate man as the monk began his prayers. It was an emotional moment, even though I had never known poor old Mr Blenkinsopp. As Father Egbert began the *De Profundis,* I felt tears coming to my eyes. The little ceremony was soon over, we shook hands and Father Egbert thanked me. Then he went away, leaving me to the police duty of dealing with a sudden death.

Looking back upon that moment, I often wonder what Sergeant Blaketon would have said if he'd entered the room during our prayers. What would he have made of a police-man kneeling beside a corpse, chanting the *De Profundis* in Latin with a Benedictine monk?

*   *   *   *

Brother Franklyn was another interesting monk who had not been ordained into the priesthood. He was studying with that in mind. He was a keen rugger player and had been captain of his school XV and of his university team. Massively built, he was as strong as an ox and coached in his sport at the local public school, which was part of the abbey complex. A real man's man, he would take his victorious team into the local pub and sup pints with them in the cause of a just celebration. He liked a good sing-song too and knew most of the popular rugger songs.

His hobby, when not playing rugby football or chanting at Evensong, was breeding white doves. My knowledge of doves is poor and I am not sure of their breed, but they were beautiful, gentle creatures of purest white and they lived in a loft at the edge of the monastery's grounds. He ministered to them daily and knew them individually; he bred from them and sold the chicks to others of similar interests, and I believe his strain was noted for their excellence. He appeared to be an authority on the subject and judged at local shows.

Around April one year, I was off duty with influenza when the telephone rang one Sunday morning. Mary answered it, and came to me after dealing with the call.

"That was Brother Franklyn," she explained, and the expression on her face told me something was wrong. Lying in bed with red eyes and a running nose, there was little I could do for the monk, but I asked what had happened.

"How did you know something was wrong?" she put to me.

"Your face, darling! It tells a million stories. What's happened to upset you?"

"Brother Franklyn's doves," she said softly. "You know them?"

"Sure," I smiled through my running eyes. Everyone knew of the doves, for they flew around the village, their wings whistling as they twisted and turned overhead, as if by some spoken command.

"Somebody's killed them," she said, with tears in her eyes. "Most of them, anyway."

"Killed them?" I cried.

She nodded. "Yes, last night, during the night. They broke into one of his lofts and they've strangled them all, wrung their necks and smashed the unhatched eggs."

"Poor Franklyn," was all I could say. "All of them?"

"No, just one of the lofts, the big one. He's got the little loft left, untouched. He says he can breed again."

"What a bloody awful thing to do." I was angry and upset at the cruelty of the persons who did this.

"He'd phoned Ashfordly but got no reply, so he rang us, just to alert the police."

"You'd explain I was off duty with flu?"

"Yes, so I said I would ring Ashfordly Police Station as soon as I knew someone was in."

"There's not a lot anyone can do now, unless someone saw the culprits," I said. "Does he think the bastards will come back and have another go at his loft?"

"I'm sure the possibility was on his mind," she told me.

"O.K. Do your best to raise someone at Ashfordly. I'd love to catch the thugs that did this, and do the same to them."

"That's not allowed." She shook a finger at me. "Thugs can misbehave, but not policemen."

An hour later, the telephone rang again and I heard Mary's voice from my resting place upstairs, but I could not distinguish her words. She came up to me, announced the caller had been Brother Franklyn and that he'd changed his mind about requesting police action.

"That's typical of a monk!" I almost shouted through my thick throat. "Somebody does him a favour like that, kills all his livestock, destroys a loft that's taken years to accumulate and what's he do? He'll go into the Abbey Church and pray for them to be forgiven! And the vandals will escape Scot free!"

I laid in bed for a further three days until I felt fit enough to venture from the room. I spent a couple of days finding my feet and my increasing strength, and I returned to work three days after that. It would be another two or three days later when I found myself on a foot patrol near the Abbey of Maddleskirk. The first person I saw walking towards me, *en route* from the post office, was Brother Franklyn.

"Good morning, Brother," I hailed him. "Good to see you."

"And you, Nicholas," he smiled broadly. "Have you recovered from your bout of 'flu?"

"Yes, all clear now. It's good to be out and about. I hate being confined to bed."

"I'm sorry I rang you about my doves when you were ill. I had no idea, or I wouldn't have troubled you."

"You weren't to know," I assured him. "I was only sorry you changed your mind about calling the police."

"I called in the heat of the moment," he said. "After I'd discovered the carnage, the police were the first people who came to mind."

We strolled together along the road in front of the magnificent abbey and he said, "I'd like to talk about it. Fancy a beer?"

"I'd love one," so he took me into the monastery guest room where he furnished me with an earthenware pint pot full of deliciously cool beer. He had one too, then told his tale.

"After I'd tried to contact the police at Ashfordly, I rang your home and found you were ill. On reflection, that was a good thing – from my point of view," he qualified his remark. "It gave me time to cool off, to reconsider my action. I had a long hard think about what had happened and decided to call off the police. After all, what could you do? The culprits had long since gone and even if you had any idea of who they

were, you'd have a most difficult job proving it, for court
purposes. There'd be a lot of work for nothing, so I cancelled
your official involvement."

"I wanted to get my hands on those vandals." I sipped the
beer and it was delightful.

"And me," he smiled. "And me. Oh, I wanted to get my
hands on them too, and wring their necks!" and he clenched
his huge fists about his pint pot.

"Why call it off then?" I asked him.

"You are a trustworthy man, aren't you?" he asked me
suddenly. "I can trust you – I can talk to you in confidence,
even on delicate matters?"

I wondered what on earth was coming now. "Of course," I
assured him.

He drew a deep breath. "Well, Nick," he spoke seriously.
"It was like this," and he proceeded to tell me this story.

It seemed he'd been very concerned about his second loft
and had a gut feeling that the vandals would return for an
attempt upon that one. He'd discussed this with his pals in
the school rugger XV who'd been incensed and who had
produced a plan of action. The entire school rugger team and
reserves would lie in wait for the killers the following
Saturday night. At first, Franklyn had been reluctant to agree
but he knew his players were furious about the death of his
birds, and they might allow it to affect their playing. This
could purge it from their systems. So he agreed, in the
interests of the game.

They had examined the area about the loft and had
worked out the likely parking places for the villains' vehicles.
Having done this, they had evolved a plan to deal with one or
more unofficial cars that might arrive in the area. Once the
passengers had left any vehicle, they would let down the tyres
and remove the rotor arm, thus effectively immobilising the
vehicle. They would then wait until the culprits were approaching the loft; at that stage, the team would pounce.
They would set about dealing with the ruffians as only a
rugby XV can.

That was the plan.

According to Brother Franklyn, the villains did arrive.
Around one-thirty in the morning, a car crept into the

grounds of Maddleskirk Abbey, parked behind a wall and four youths emerged. This had been spotted by one of the concealed members who had promptly activated their 'peace plan'. They called it that because the dove is the emblem of peace.

Without exception, those boys were massive, powerful youths of seventeen or eighteen, and one of them removed the rotor arm of the car. Once the invaders were out of earshot, two of them let down the tyres, and so the trespassers were marooned within the grounds of the abbey. Meanwhile, the marauding gang had made their approach to the small loft as anticipated, although their movements were now monitored every inch of the way. And as they had begun their climb up the steps, their approach had been completely cut off. They found themselves surrounded by twenty powerful youths, all hell-bent on having a whale of a time at the expense of some ugly villains.

Brother Franklyn was in bed at the time, which I felt was a very diplomatic move because he could justifiably claim not to be involved in this episode. The four villains had been given 'the treatment'; they had been severely thrashed to say the least, and had then been cast fully clothed into the slime-covered disused outdoor swimming pool. After an enforced swim there, they had been allowed out, and their shoes had been removed. They had then been sent on their way home to the nearby market town of Harrowby, a walk of ten miles or so. It was rough treatment for a set of cowardly rogues. After minutes, their shoes had been returned, but it was still a long, long walk.

"So there we are," smiled Brother Franklyn. "That's what happened."

"I don't want to know about it," I said.

"They daren't tell you, dare they? You'd have them for killing my birds?"

"I would, but you'd best not mention this to a soul!" I advised.

"I won't, I won't," he breathed.

"I must be going, Brother," I stood up to leave. "Thanks for the beer, and thanks for telling me about it. I feel better now – my mind is at rest. Justice has been done.

Really, they have received their punishment, haven't they? Goodbye."

"Peace be with you," he said, showing me the door.

Ten

That year, Christmas arrived all too quickly. It seemed but a week or two since our arrival at Aidensfield and the changing weather, the darkening nights, the cooling of the air had descended upon us almost without warning. The clocks had gone back an hour, the summer birds had left our valleys and the land had reverted to its dullest clothing. It was as if the countryside had gone to sleep, and I was reminded of Keats who wrote:

"Ah, bitter chill it was!
The owl, for all his feathers, was a-cold;
The hare limp'd trembling through the frozen grass,
And silent was the flock in woolly fold."

But the countryside was far from trembling, even though the owl might be cold and the hare trembling. Like the dormant plants and the animals who hunt for survival, the weather means little to the policemen of Great Britain. They must work throughout the seasons – it means cold nights, wet feet, chilled hands and a longing for warm soup, hot coffee and cosy firesides. It means, after eight hours of frost-laden night duty, the heaven that is a snug bed containing a warm, soft woman.

Out there in the great chilly wilderness that is North Yorkshire, the work of the policeman must go on which means that policemen must tolerate the cold, and they must tremble, like the hare, in the chilly atmosphere. Motor-cycling in such conditions was appalling, so I took my car as often as possible, hiding it from the sergeants behind hay-stacks and in the yards of friendly farmers. I could therefore embark upon rapid foot patrols of my area to keep myself warm. I risked being called on my official radio, for I had

171

none in the car, but I could always plead that I was in an area of poor reception, or engaged upon enquiries about current crime or missing persons, an act which took me away from the radio. In any case, I continued to make hourly points at telephone kiosks consequently I was never long out of contact with my Divisional Headquarters.

This highly unofficial strategy meant that my winter patrols weren't too bad. I took care to keep warm, I had lots of friendly calling places around my beat and I made sure that I had lots of enquiries to undertake, enquiries which took me indoors to sit beside warm fires and to enjoy numerous cups of tea and coffee, and/or glasses of proffered spirits.

Work under those conditions had considerable appeal, and I was aware of the old saying, "A good policeman never gets wet."

At home, the children were beginning to realise it was a season with something extra to offer. Father Christmas was very much alive in our family and even though a police house chimney is perhaps narrower than most, I ensured that letters were posted into its lofty darkness. I'm something of a traditionalist in that respect, for I love the joy that Father Christmas brings to youngsters during that season of goodwill and plenty. To abolish Christmas would be to abolish a slice of childhood.

Happily, by this time we had found a baby-sitter in a million, a steadfast lady of the moors who stood no nonsense from anybody, man, woman, child or animal, but who would sit till dawn if necessary and who would let us know in plain terms if something did not suit her. Her philosophy about children was "If they yell, I'll skelp 'em". Mrs Quarry was a treasure. It was fortunate we had found her before the Christmas season which, incidentally, begins at the end of October and develops into a hectic and expensive round of dinners, dances, parties and other associated functions.

My shifts did not allow me to attend every function, nor did my pocket, so we opted for the Ashfordly Police Christmas Dinner-Dance, held in the second week of December at a local hotel. Sergeants Bairstow and Blaketon had organised it with volunteers from the other lads in that town, and it was to raise funds for police widows and orphans. Being a late arrival in the district, I found myself free from official dance duties that night.

Mary and I decided to go along and to make this our sole Christmas fling. One reason was that we were hard up, a situation that has been with me ever since,· for I had had a brain-storm a few months earlier and had purchased a brand-new car. What on earth possessed me to do such a thing on a police constable's pittance, with three youngsters and a fourth nearly there, I'll never know. But I had done it. It was a red Hillman saloon and it cost me, brand-new, £609 on the road. It was the first and last new car I've ever purchased, and it ran for well over 100,000 miles, We loved it. Naturally, we took it all over before the frosts and ice played havoc with the highways of the region, and it was our Christmas present to each other. For that reason, we had to economise, therefore we settled for one Yuletide function.

Mrs Quarry insisted that she baby-sat for us that night, even though the dance did not conclude until 2 am. We agreed to this. Mary had the statutory hair-do, but had to make do with an existing dress, while I dug out my only dark suit, brushed it, pulled in my belly and decided I must wear it. I had nothing else. Armed with a pocket full of cash, we left the children in the capable hands of Mrs Quarry and sallied forth into Ashfordly, very excited and looking forward to the dance. The car went beautifully and we arrived at Ashfordly at 7.30 for dancing at eight. We adjourned to the bar where we met our colleagues and friends, and in no time the function was going with the proverbial swing.

A tombola room was set aside from the dance hall and it was separated from the bar by a passage. It was like Aladdin's cave, piled high with prizes all donated by local people. There were bottles of spirits, boxes of chocolates, wines, Christmas cakes, game birds, silverware, glasses, cutlery *et al.* It looked almost like a display of wedding presents; we played tombola and won a box of chocolates.

Alwyn Foxton was the man in charge of this department and he said, "You can leave your prize here if you like, Nick. It'll save worrying about it during the dancing."

And so, like many other winners, we left our trophy on the table behind the glittering display and went off to enjoy the dance. The floor was excellent, sprung to take the rhythmic movement of skilled dancers, while the walls were decorated with original oil paintings by a local artist. They depicted our moorlands with purple heather and blue skies. High above was the buffet supper, served on a balcony which ran around the room and from where the diners could sit and view the dancing below. Supper was to be served at nine-thirty, a sit-down buffet.

The night disappeared in a haze of enjoyment and warmth. At functions of this kind, there is always so much to do, so many old friends to greet and to chat with, so much entertainment and so much chatting-up-of-pretty-women. The time flies without anyone realising. The leader of the little five-piece orchestra announced that it was time to eat, and we all adjourned upstairs for the feast of a lifetime. We were back within half-an-hour, to resume our merry-making.

Then I spotted Sergeant Bairstow, looking very harassed.

"Ah, Nicholas!" he spotted me in the middle of a Boston Two-Step. "Have you a minute?"

I led Mary to the side, bowed my ear against the noise of the music and heard him say, "It's bloody embarrassing, is this. But did you play tombola earlier this evening?"

"Yes, Mary won a box of chocolates. Black Magic, I think."

"Well," he coughed and ran his hand through his untidy hair. "Somebody's pinched the lot. They've cleaned out the whole bloody room – there's nothing left."

"That *is* embarrassing," I whispered.

"A lot of the stuff hadn't been won, so that's not too important, but what about all those prizes, like yours, that had been put to one side, for safe keeping? We'll have to replace them."

"Forget ours," I said. "But you can't replace them, Sergeant, can you? You don't know what they were. And if you announce what's happened, everyone will start claiming bottles of whisky or silverware, won't they?"

"Aye," he said dejectedly. "They will. We'll have to buy them all replacement prizes, and that'll ruin us. It'll take all our profit – and more."

"Why not announce that the tombola room has closed, as all the prizes have been won," I suggested. "Then ask the

prize winner to see you, in person, to claim their prizes before
they leave. Ask them individually what they won, and then
tell them what's happened. Offer to buy a substitute tomorrow. I'll bet a lot of them will dismiss the affair and forgo
their prize."

"I hope you're right," he sighed. "What a bloody thing to
happen. I hope the Press doesn't hear about it."

They didn't, or if they did, they did not print anything. I
was still amused by the incident as we left the dance at 2 am.
By that time, word of the theft had percolated to most of the
revellers and they thought it hilarious. Not many of them
made claims upon the prize list, and if I know those folks,
there'd be no false claims. The final outcome was not unpleasant, and we maintained a bank balance.

Outside that night, however, a covering of seasonal snow
had fallen and it lay about two inches deep, "reg'lar away" as
the locals term it. In other words, it was a level covering of
that depth, unhampered by winds. For that reason, I drove
with extreme care in my new car, the drink I'd enjoyed earlier
having long since vanished from my system. The dancing and
the superb meal had nullified the effects of any alcohol, and
so I manoeuvred my shining vehicle through the forests and
lanes as I neared my house on the hill top.

And then, as I negotiated a stiff bend about a mile from
home, I felt the front wheels misbehave. The car refused to
turn the corner. It was determined to travel in a straight line
towards the tall hedge before me, and in spite of my wrest-
ling with brakes and steering, it continued along its predetermined path. It mounted the verge on the nearside,
climbed steeply towards its summit and threw light powdery
snow in all directions. Then very gently, oh so very gently, it
twisted across its path and toppled onto its side. My side. And
there I was, sliding along a snow covered highway on the
clean red doors of my new car. Mary was on top of me,
cushioned by my body as we careered onwards with the
engine roaring and the lights reflecting from the white
expanse before me, and so close to my eyes. Everything
seemed to be happening in slow motion and I was trying to
lift my head away from my door window in case it shattered.
I worried about our unborn baby too and all kinds of things

flashed through my mind as we came gently to rest some yards further along.

"Are you all right?" I asked Mary, who was sitting on my head.

"Yes, are you?" came her voice from somewhere above.

"Fine," I tried to appear calm. She was moving somewhere above me and I saw her feet on the door beside my head. She was opening the window of the door above her, and once she'd achieved this, I helped her out. I switched off the engine but the lights were still blazing and there was an ominous smell of petrol. Then, in a blaze of light, another car pulled up.

"Have you had an accident, old boy?" asked a splendid voice.

"No, I always park like this." I wasn't feeling too affable, but he roared with laughter, expressed pleasure that we were not injured and offered to topple my Hillman back onto its wheels. With three more helpers from his car, we easily returned mine onto its four wheels and a superficial examination revealed very little damage. The thick snow had cushioned our fall and the only damage appeared to be the door handles on my side, plus a few minor scratches. I thanked him and off he went, chortling at the delight of finding a policeman in such a compromising situation after the dance. He laughed again at my ungrateful remark and I promised to buy him a drink if I saw him at another function.

I drove the final yards home and the car performed very well. It was very slightly damaged.

"Did you have a nice time?" asked Mrs Quarry as Mary entered, covered in snow, with her hair awry, her feet soaking and a patch of dirt on her cheek.

"Wonderful," she said. "Yes, wonderful."

*   *   *   *

With my car at the village garage getting its doors corrected and re-sprayed, I had to return briefly to the chilly motor-cycle for some of my winter patrols. With ice always a possibility on the roads, I was never fully confident upon that machine; having only two wheels puts one at considerable risk and I think the car accident had shaken me more than I cared to admit. Nonetheless, I managed to patrol my beat in that wintry weather and I did not suffer any further mishaps.

As is customary on a rural policeman's beat, one is fêted with alacrity during the festive season, and I had offers of wine, Christmas cake, spirits, beer and frumenty. Because it was the Christmas season, I accepted these positive indications of appreciation, although I took great care never to over-indulge, especially with alcoholic drinks. If I took a drink, I walked home. I found this to be the safest way of patrolling and therefore the motor-cycle found itself spending more and more time in the garage. I patrolled my beat on foot, having in mind the very generous and very persuasive rural folk.

Christmas is a happy time for a rural policeman, and it should also be a happy time for his 'parishioners'. This came to mind one Friday evening as I patrolled Elsinby on foot. It was bitterly cold and there was a hint of snow in the air, coupled with what Yorkshiremen call a "lazy wind". It goes through you – it is too lazy to go round. I had walked from Aidensfield into Elsinby and was therefore quite snug in my winter uniform. I made my ten o'clock point at the telephone kiosk and was about to leave when the phone rang. It was Sergeant Blaketon.

"Ah!" The relief was evident in his voice. "Got you, Rhea. We've just had a telephone call from a lady in Elsinby. She's complaining about the noise at the pub. Very loud singing, apparently. It's disturbing the neighbourhood. Go and sort them out, will you? Tell them to shut up. I know it's the festive season, but we don't want complaints."

"Yes, Sergeant."

I walked the few hundred yards and as I approached the Hopbind Inn, I could hear lusty voices rising from it. The place was undoubtedly in fine song and the cheery atmosphere gave me a feeling of loneliness and isolation. I wished I was in there right now, warm and snug, with friendly folk and a nice drink. But the din was awful! I could hear a familiar tune whose title escaped me; it could be heard well away from the premises and there was little wonder the lady had complained.

I walked into the busy pub and George, the landlord, greeted me with a smile. Clearly, he was pleased with the music.

"By, that's a bit of grand singing," he clutched a full pint pot as he beamed with pleasure.

"It's too good, George," I shouted above the noise. "We've had a complaint. Somebody's rung our office at Ashfordly to complain about it. I've just had Sergeant Blaketon asking you to shut up."

"You're joking!" he gasped.

"I'm not," I said seriously. "They making a hell of a racket, you know. I could hear them half way up the street."

"But Nick, listen to them!" he pleaded and he held up a finger to indicate silence. I listened to the tune that came from the bar. It was a fine version of "The old rugged cross", a popular Methodist hymn sung regularly in these parts. For the Methodists of this region, it was almost an anthem.

"Hymns?" I asked.

"Aye, hymns. It's the carol singers." He lowered his voice. "They were singing out there and it's bloody cold tonight. Everybody in the bar invited them inside – they're chapel folks, Nick, and they don't touch a drop. They're just singing hymns and carols, that's all, inside my pub instead of on the street."

I laughed aloud. "If they thought they'd been the subject of a complaint about singing in the pub, they'd never live it down!"

"They wouldn't," he agreed. "Can you do summat about it?"

"I don't know who made the complaint," I had to tell him, "and I daren't ring Blaketon to tell him the truth. To him, a noise is a noise, whoever makes it and for whatever reason. All I know is that the caller was a woman."

"Oh, it will be Miss Allison just around the corner. She often grumbles and she's got the telephone in. She's the only woman living alone along there."

"I'll see if it was her," I offered. I went to her cottage and knocked. It was about ten fifteen by this time and she answered quickly. Behind me, the strains of "Silent Night" were now ringing forth.

"Did you ring our office at Ashfordly, Miss Allison?" I asked.

"I did, Mr Rhea, yes I did. I'm sorry if I am a nuisance, but the noise from the Hopbind was getting too much."

"It's the chapel carol singers," I told her. "Listen, they're there now."

Standing together on her doorstep, we listened to the verses of that popular carol as they filled the chill air of this December night.

"Oh dear, I thought it was someone in the pub," she blushed. "I had no idea it was carol singers."

"It is carol singers, but they are in the pub," I corrected her, and explained about the chapel folks, now firmly installed in the bar and singing their hearts out beside the regulars. She burst into laughter.

"Oh, dear, that's marvellous, isn't it? Really marvellous. I'm so sorry I complained . . . Do they know I complained?"

"No one knows," I assured her, "except me and George. I'm going back to put his mind at rest. Can they continue like that? It closes at eleven and besides, there are many chapel folk in there who will soon want to be going home."

"Thank you for telling me." She sounded sincere, and I got the impression she was wistful.

As she made to close the door, I said, "I'm going back, Miss Allison. Would you like to come across and hear them for yourself?"

"Oh, I'm not a drinker, you know. I never go into pubs."

"Neither are they. They're singers."

"Do you think I should? I mean, it's not the thing for a woman to go into a public house unaccompanied."

"I will accompany you. You could stand in the passage with me and listen to the carols."

"Thank you," she smiled, and in a second she had on a warm coat and a scarf. George was delighted and by the time we arrived, the singers, chapel folks and regulars, were in top form with "Oh Come All Ye Faithful".

I could inform Sergeant Blaketon that I had dealt with the complaint and that all parties were satisfied with my action. But I did wonder what the Catholics and Anglicans would do to cap this one!

*   *   *   *

George Boston, his wife and son occupied Low Laithes Farm. Its fields spread smoothly across a lush and green part of the valley below my lounge window and in moments of silent reflection, I would often stand at that window to gaze across the dale far below. My view looked south across the deep rift in the hills where ranging conifers decorated the slopes. Christmas tree thieves would be a menace in there about now; I'd have to arrange patrols during the darkened hours. Lonely farmsteads dotted those slopes and their lights twinkled at night, lighting my view like glow-worms in the undergrowth. I could look down upon the spread of the whole dale.

Boston's farm provided an everlasting frontage to my view. There were times his spread was hidden in the mists of autumn. Sometimes his farm was totally obscured and sometimes I could see only the tops of the trees and the caps of spindly telegraph poles protruding from the dense white blanket. At other times the Boston farm lay revealed in all its symmetrical wonder, with neat walls, trimmed hedges and the tidiest farmyard for miles around. Even his animals seemed tidy – sometimes I could have sworn they grazed in drilled ranks.

From my vantage point, I could watch George at work and I began to recognise his wife's daily routine. White smoke spiralling from her chimney told me whether or not it was going to be a fine day, but it also told me whether Mary Boston was baking, washing the clothes or going out for the day. If she was baking, the fire would be lit early to heat the fireside oven she continued to use to such tasty advantage; if it was wash-day, the wash-house fire would belch forth a darker smoke from behind the main house, while a day's outing meant no smoke until later in the day, usually around tea-time.

The farm buildings were gathered about the dwelling-house like pups around a loving mother; they were homely, warm and inviting, so friendly and yet so plain. Their construction and furnishings were simple and provided a life without complications. The fields were the same, always neat, always well tended and up to date with whatever crop George had decided to produce. The place reeked of rural contentment.

Sometimes I stood at the window, wondering if the Bostons bothered about the village bobby being so high above them with such a splendid view of their territory. Did they have the feeling they were being watched? Did they think the village constable was spying on them? Did they feel that my binoculars were upon *them,* and not upon the wildlife that lived about their premises? It was like standing on a mountain top and observing the minutiae of life in a valley far below; but George's life and mine were really no part of each other.

My first visit to his farm was some six or eight weeks after my arrival, and it had been a routine check of his stock register. When a farmer bought stock, he had to enter details in a register, including facts like the date and time of purchase, the place they were purchased, the number of animals and a brief description. Cows and pigs were the chief livestock of this area and it was my job to ensure their entries were correct. If an outbreak of disease occurred, it would have to be traced to its source, consequently those records were vital.

My second visit was for a totally different purpose. It was strictly official and it reminded me of the risks attached to the nationwide practice of giving Christmas presents to village policemen. Policemen are always conscious of attempts to bribe them during their duties, and the acceptance of gifts, however small, is fraught with danger. Police Regulations are specific upon the subject. Some superiors interpreted these rules so rigidly that acceptance of a cup of tea on duty was seen as the acceptance of a present. Reliable sources of tea were therefore jealously guarded by policemen.

This second visit occurred on Christmas Day, when such temptations were placed before me. I had been off duty during Christmas Eve and my Christmas Day duties were from 10 am until 6 pm. This suggested a daytime patrol of the village and its surrounding area, and meant I was always available for despatch to any incident, large or small. In reality, it meant I stayed at home with my family, always on the understanding that if anything did happen, I must go out and deal with it. On Christmas Day therefore, I sat around the house in my uniform shirt and trousers, hoping nothing would happen. This system gave me Christmas Day at home.

Shortly after ten o'clock that morning, my telephone rang. It was P.C. Jim Finn from Ashfordly.

"Nick, I'm sorry, but we've got a job for you."

"I was out of bed," I laughed. The children had seen to that – Father Christmas had roused them about three this morning, from which time sleep had been impossible.

"It's not serious," Jim was telling me. "A hit-and-run accident in the early hours. Damage only, no injuries. We didn't get you up at the crack of dawn, but it needs attention."

It seemed that a worshipper had attended Midnight Mass at Maddleskirk Abbey. Mass had concluded about 1.15 am and the worshipper had turned his car towards Aidensfield, aiming for his home. Unfortunately, some of the local pubs had been making merry at the same time, and had thrown out their faithful just as the Abbey was ejecting its regulars.

A small Morris Minor had hurtled along the narrow lane between Maddleskirk and Aidensfield. According to an eye-witness, it had been driven erratically and had collided with a nice new car belonging to the said worshipper. The Morris had not troubled to stop, but had careered out of sight amidst a rending of metal and a tinkling of broken glass. The eye-witness, another home-going worshipper, had seen this incident from the relative safety of a wood, into which he had had the presence of mind to leap as the offending Morris approached. Nonetheless, he had had the sense to note the registration number of the Morris.

"So," concluded P.C. Finn. "There's a useful 'Careless Driving' for you, a 'Fail to Stop' and a 'Fail to Report'."

"Who was driving the Morris?" I asked.

"Dunno. I can give you its number, but the Taxation Offices are closed. They won't be able to supply the keeper's name until after the holiday. Maybe you know the owner?"

When he told me the number, I knew it was a local lad. The car belonged to George Boston's son, a lanky twenty-year-old called Samuel Victor. This revelation meant I was faced with a rather unpleasant Christmas Day task. However, sentiment and seasonal jollifications cannot be allowed to infringe upon the execution of one's lawful duty, so I put on my uniform tunic and cap, told my wife where I was heading and said I'd be back for lunch.

Although I often felt I could toss a pebble from my garden
into the stackyard of Low Laithes Farm, it was about a mile
from my house when using the conventional route. I decided
to walk and enjoyed the clear, crisp morning air, with just a
hint of frost. There was a suggestion of snow too, for snow
packs were forming around the horizon and there was the
distinctive smell of oncoming snow. It is a peculiar smell, one
which is recognised by countrymen. I knew that smell. Snow
was on its way and would fall before long.

I arrived at the gate of Low Laithes Farm just before
eleven, having passed the time of day with one or two
residents *en route*. I touched the latch and it swung open. They
call this type of latch a hunting sneck, a wooden affair
peculiar to this part of England and perhaps designed to be
drawn by the lighest of touches from a riding crop, or by Miss
Fiona's pony. It was simply a long wooden bolt, hanging from
short chains and carved with nicks. When the gate is open, it
hangs free but once closed, it is very secure. The Boston dogs
began their well practised barking and, with my arrival thus
announced, I walked across the clean farmyard, with its area
of grooved concrete as clean as the front path of any semi-
detached house in the land. This farm even lacked the traditional midden, a heap of dung and household waste which
was once so familiar at the front door of every farmstead. I
knocked on the kitchen door and Mrs Boston, a plump
attractive woman in a flowered apron, opened it. She was
smiling a welcome.

"I saw you coming, Mr Rhea. Fancy calling on Christmas
Day?" and at that, she adopted a slightly worried frown.

"E'll have cum for 'is duck," growled a voice from inside
the kitchen. "T'bobby allus comes for 'is duck on Christmas
Day. Fetch 'im in."

"Well," I began . . .

"Don't stand oot there, it's cawd," said George's voice.
"Bring t'lad in."

I entered and removed my cap, and was immediately inside
the farm kitchen. A friendly fire warmed the room, casting
bright and flickering glows of red across the furnishings, the
tiled floor and the beamed ceiling so brown and stained with
age. Meat hooks decorated the ceiling and horse brasses were

crudely nailed to much of the woodwork. George Boston sat in a Windsor chair, the cushion bulging between the uprights. He wore a thick tweed jacket of mottled green and brown, a fawn waistcoat and heavy corduroy trousers, polished with regular wear and tear. His feet wore battered but cosy slippers, one of which had a hole in the toe, and a pet cur lay at his feet. Its head rested on the fender almost within reach of falling cinders, while its body sprawled across the thick clip hearth rug. It didn't rouse at my entry, and George didn't leave his chair.

"Noo then, lad," he beamed. "Thoo'll 'ave cum for thy Christmas duck, eh?"

"No, I haven't," I had to say. I knew nothing of such an arrangement. "It's about something else, Mr Boston."

"Get 'im 'is duck oot o' t'larder, Mary. Let's git this bit owered afoore he spoils things."

"No," I insisted. "Please, you mustn't. I'm here on business – you'll not want to give me a duck when you hear what I've got to say."

He studied me for a few moments and said, "Oh, it's like that is it? Sit down then," and he indicated a chair at the table. I put my cap on the scrubbed wooden top and Mrs Boston produced a mug of tea from somewhere. This was their break time, 'lowance time as they called it.

"Give 'im summat stronger than that, Mary," insisted George.

I held up my hand. "No, wait, please. I must tell you why I'm here."

"This lad's nut gahin ti be bribed, is he?" smiled the genial farmer. "Well, lad, oot wiv it. What's up? It must be summat important to drag you oot looking serious on Christmas Day."

I told him about last night's incident, or this morning's to be precise, and he listened without a word. Mrs Boston stood close to me, listening carefully and sipping from her mug which she clutched with both hands. I told them the story in what I hoped was a clear manner and left the identification of the alleged offender until the end.

"That Morris car," I said. "It bore the same registration number as your son's car," and I quoted the number.

"Aye," he said. "That's oor lad's car and no mistake. Is onnybody hurt?"

"No," I said to his relief. "Just minor damage to both vehicles."

"If he'd stopped, it might 'ave been sorted out there and then."

"Possibly," I agreed, wondering if Samuel had been drunk at the time.

"What happens next then?"

"I'd like to see the car."

"Me an' all," and he slipped his feet into a pair of waiting wellington boots and led me through the back of the house, the cur following without any bidding. We traversed a cattle shed or two with cows ruminating noisily in their winter quarters, the heat of their bodies warming the entire complex. Finally, we entered an outbuilding which served as a garage.

"There she is," he pointed to a car.

Out came my official notebook as I circled the little car, looking for signs of recent damage. I found them; the front offside wing had been dented and the surface paint was fractured. The bumper was twisted and the headlamp glass was broken, most of it being missing. There were clean, rust-free scratches along the doors too, and also along the rear wing, all on the driver's side. It had clearly been in a recent collision. I noted this damage and then, taking out my pocket knife, lifted a sample of paint from the damaged part of the car. I carefully placed this in a plastic envelope and then, upon the damaged portion of the car, I located an alien colour, a dull red paint. I guessed this had been transferred from the other vehicle during their contact, so I lifted this and placed it in another envelope.

"What's all this business for?" George asked with genuine interest.

"I might have to prove it was him," I said. "I have taken a control sample of the paintwork from Samuel's car, and another piece bearing a different coloured paint. That shows he touched something else, something bearing that colour of paint. We'll do the same with the other chap's car, then we will get our forensic wizards to examine all the pieces. They'll tell us whether the two cars were ever in contact with one another. I reckon they'll say 'yes'."

"You fellers leave nowt to chance, do you?"

"No," I said. "We don't."

After I had noted the excise licence details, I said, "I'd like to see Sam now. Where is he?"

"He'll be in these buildings. I'll shout him."

He bellowed Sam's name and soon the lad appeared looking pale and dishevelled, the legacy of his night out. He was very tall and thin, a serious-faced lad but pleasant to deal with.

"Now, Sam." I did not smile.

"Hello, Mr Rhea," and his eyes did not meet mine.

"You know why I'm here?"

"Aye."

"It's your car?" I had to ask the formal question for evidential purposes.

"Aye."

"And you were driving it from Maddleskirk towards Aidensfield in the early hours of this morning, past the Abbey about quarter-past-one?"

"Aye."

George interrupted us to address his son. "Leeakster, lad, when thoo's involved in summat like a traffic accident, thoo's got ti stop and tell t'folks who's there who thoo is . . ."

"Aye, Ah know," said Samuel, "but Ah was scared."

"Drunk, mair like," snapped his father.

"Ah'd had a few, not too many, not enough to stop me driving."

"Thoo'll nut be having t'lad for drinking and driving, Mr Rhea?"

"No," I said to his relief. This was before the days of the breathalyser and besides, this youth was stone cold sober now. "He's not drunk now, and I can't prove what he was like when this happened, can I?"

George smiled.

"Come inti t'house then, both on you."

We followed him inside and he produced a bottle of whisky. "It's Christmas Day, Mr Rhea, so thoo'll have a noggin wiv us?"

"Aye," I said, "I will, but I must see this lad's papers first – insurance, driving licence, test certificate." I hoped they were all in order, for I didn't want to get Samuel into deeper trouble.

"Get 'em, Sam."

I was relieved to find they were all correct, and I sat at the table to note their particulars in my notebook. As I worked, Samuel plonked a huge glass of whisky before me. It was neat and there must have been a third of a pint.

"Sup it up, lad, it'll warm thoo nicely."

"Samuel," I addressed him before I lifted my glass. "I've got to report you for various offences – it will probably mean an appearance at Eltering Magistrates' Court."

"Can't thoo settle it oot o' court?" asked George.

"This is a criminal court, it's not a civil case," I tried to explain the difference. "We've had a formal complaint about Sam's driving, so I've no choice. I've got to submit my report and Sam will get a summons in due course."

"It won't mean prison, will it?" The lad's eyes were wide and fearful.

"No, a fine perhaps, a smallish one. It's your first offence," and I tried to put the situation in its right perspective.

"Ah'll say it was my fault, 'cos it was," offered Samuel, white-faced and obviously worried. "Ah should 'ave stopped, Mr Rhea; Ah was bloody daft not to."

"Fair enough. Now listen to what I'm reporting you for," I advised. "First, there's bound to be careless driving. Then you failed to stop after an accident, and you failed to report it to the police as soon as practicable."

"Three, eh?" counted his father. "Three offences."

"Three," I confirmed.

"Not drunk driving?"

"No," I said once more. "I've no evidence to suggest he was drunk."

"Nobody said I was?" Samuel's statement was phrased like a question.

"Nobody suggested anything of the sort, Sam. It won't enter my report. You panicked, that's all."

"Aye," he smiled. "Fair enough."

"Thoo's a lucky lad, Sam," commented his father.

"You'll get a summons in about three weeks," I told him.

"Serves the young bugger right," said George when I'd finished. "Ah've had a go at him for gahin oot late and driving home. Yon pub needs checking, lad, for boozing late."

"It's not on my beat, Mr Boston, but I'll have words with the sergeant."

"Aye, well, sup that whisky. This is Christmas, thoo knaws."

Samuel and Mrs Boston joined us and we chatted as we always had before this incident. We talked of nothing in particular for this was just another friendly chat between the village bobby and one of his farming community. What we had discussed ten minutes earlier was now over and done with. I stayed longer than I intended and had two more massive whiskies. I found the room beginning to move about me, so I made a pathetic attempt to leave.

"It's a good job thoo's walking back, lad," George laughed. "Ah hope thy missus has a nice heavy dinner ready. Thoo'll need summat to sober thyself up, 'specially if t'sergeant turns up."

"She's busy with the dinner now," I muttered incoherently, aiming for the door. "Thankshh for being sho co-operative."

"Hod on, lad, thoo's forgotten summat," George called me back.

"Forgotten?" I wondered if I had left my cap, but it was perched on my head in approximately the right position. I looked at George. He was holding a massive, dressed duck, ready for the oven.

"It's thy Christmas duck, tak it."

"No, I couldn't, not after reporting Sshamuel."

"Oor Sam was a bloody fool; he's lucky he's not been takken off t'road for ever, drunk driving or summat warse. Tak this duck – it's thine."

"I can't," I managed to say, "I musshn't – I cannot accept gifts, it's againssht the rules."

"Who said it was for thoo?" he questioned me. "It's not."

"Then who issh it for?" I asked stupidly.

"Thy wife and kids," he smiled. "There's no law to say Ah can't give thy missus and bairns a duck, is there?"

I left, bearing the huge bare duck beneath my arm as I

wound my erratic way back up the hill and into my cosy house. I was just in time for dinner and spent the afternoon getting over that spell of duty. I sat around, at first in a haze of noise and fun, and then in a clearer atmosphere as I played with the children and their new toys. Nothing else turned up, except a sprinkling of snow. As George Boston would have said, "It snew on Christmas Day, just a strinkling."

But that 'strinkling' became a steady snowfall and I could see the features of his farm gradually vanishing in a desert of white. Walls disappeared against a background of pure white and I was reminded of the lines of Robert Bridges' poem, 'London Snow',

"Hushing the latest traffic of the drowsy town;
Deadening, muffling, stifling its murmurs failing;
Lazily and incessantly floating down and down:
  Silently sifting and veiling road, roof and railing;
Hiding difference, making unevenness even,
Into angles and crevices softly drifting and sailing."

With that snow, Christmas had truly arrived and the land about grew whiter as evening fell. It was a very pleasant Christmas Day.

We had the duck for New Year's Day dinner and it was truly delicious, and that Christmas and New Year, Mary received eleven pheasants, two brace of grouse, one hare, two Christmas cakes, several bottles, one umbrella and a bag of anonymous Brussels sprouts.

A month later, Samuel was fined a total of £32 and had his licence endorsed.